Aiming for the Heart of God

Rev. Kathryn L. Smith

AIMING FOR THE HEART OF GOD

By
REV. KATHRYN L. SMITH

AUTHOR OF
THERE IS FIRE IN THE BLOOD
MEET ME ON THE MOUNTAIN
I HEAR THE ROCKS FALLING
WILT THOU BE MADE WHOLE
I AM WHO GOD SAYS I AM
STARTING WITH ZERO

PUBLISHED by PARABLES
Earthly Stories with a Heavenly Meaning

Rev. Kathryn L. Smith

Aiming for the Heart of God
Rev. Kathryn L. Smith

Published By Parables
February, 2020

All Rights Reserved. No part of this book may be reproduced or utilized in any form or by any means, electronic or mechanical, including photocopying, recording, or by any information storage and retrieval system, without permission in writing from the author.

    ISBN 978-1-951497-30-9
    Printed in the United States of America

Readers should be aware that Internet Web sites offered as citations and/or sources for further information may have been changed or disappeared between the time this was written and the time it is read.

Aiming for the Heart of God

By
Rev. Kathryn L. Smith

Author of
There is Fire in the Blood
Meet Me on the Mountain
I Hear the Rocks Falling
Wilt Thou Be Made Whole
I am who God says I am
Starting With Zero

Table of Contents

7	Acknowledgments
9	Missing the Mark
13	Least Likely to Succeed
19	Is there anyone else?
29	Judas and Peter endings
35	Zealous Servants
41	God's next Hall of Faith
47	His Goodness is Running After Me
57	What do you see?
63	Stop trying so hard
75	Lending to the Lord
83	After the drought
91	Looking unto Jesus
95	Where are you in the crowd?
105	Don't worry, pray
113	Unashamed Passion
121	Works Cited
122	Author Page

Acknowledgements

It is with deep love and appreciation that I dedicate this book to Donna Naylor. She is my dearest friend. We share times of prayer and Bible study and lots of silly memories. She puts God first in everything she does. She has always been the first to read my books and she is not afraid to tell me when something is unclear or grammatically incorrect; she loves the red pen, but more than that she loves both God and me.

I deeply appreciate all those who made me the woman of faith, the minister, and the author that I am. I want to especially thank Pastor Timothy A. Naylor & Pastor Rick Naylor, who taught me what it meant to be called and how to minister. They taught me faith, and to trust in the indisputable Word of God. My pastors and other men of faith have invested in my spiritual growth and served as shepherds to my soul. I also want to express my gratitude to all the men and women whose ministries and books have shaped my faith; some of those names have faded over time, but their truths have become ingrained within my spirit; to all those who taught me and nurtured me, but were not specifically cited in this book—thank you.

Thank you to my dear husband, Buzz who patiently endured countless hours alone while I ministered or wrote. He has supported and honored my calling and prayed for me. I deeply love and appreciate the man of God that he is and the constant love that he shows me.

I want to thank the people who so kindly and consistently encouraged me, and those who have purchased and read my books.

Mostly, I want to thank the Lord Jesus Christ who loved me when I was unlovely, saved me when I was lost, called me when I was nothing and anointed me to do His work. I pray that He will be glorified and lifted high in all I have attempted for Him.

Deuteronomy 4:29 (KJV) *²⁹ But if from thence thou shalt seek the LORD thy God, thou shalt find him, if thou seek Him with all thy heart and with all thy soul.*

Missing the Mark

When I was in high school I took archery. I wasn't all that good but I pretty much learned the basics and I passed the class. I didn't lower the score of a whole team, because it was an individual sport. I improved with practice. I was there every day and I never lost an arrow. I know that isn't saying much but I do have a point. I remember that there were various techniques but the idea was to focus on the point where you wanted the arrow to land; aim to get it as close as you can to the center of the target. I was told not to look at the arrow itself, or the bow, but only at the center of the target.

As Christians, that would be a great goal for us as well. We can either hit or miss the mark spiritually, based on how closely we focus on and connect with the heart of God. There is so much in the Bible about men and women who were right on target and those who missed the target entirely.

First and foremost, if we want to touch the heart of God, we need to be looking at Him. We cannot set our sights on some achievement or program or length of time in prayer just a steady eye on the One we love. **Ephesians 2:4-10 (KJV)** *[4] But God, who is rich in mercy, for his great love wherewith he loved us, [5] Even when we were dead in sins, hath quickened us together with Christ, (by grace ye are saved;) [6] And hath raised us up together, and made us sit together in heavenly places in Christ Jesus: [7] That in the ages to come he might shew the exceeding riches of his grace in his kindness toward us through Christ Jesus. [8] For by grace are ye saved through faith; and that not of yourselves: it is the gift of God: [9] Not of works, lest any man should boast. [10] For we are his workman-ship, created in Christ Jesus unto good works, which God hath before ordained that we should walk in them.*

Our Father wants us in touch with Him. He is not hiding or making it hard for us; He is always accessible to us. He loves us, so if we just bask in that love and give it back we are on the right track. **I John 4:17-19 (KJV)** *17 Herein is our love made perfect, that we may have boldness in the day of judgment: because as he is, so are we in this world. 18 There is no fear in love; but perfect love casteth out fear: because fear hath torment. He that feareth is not made perfect in love. 19 We love him, because he first loved us.*

In sign language there are two signs for sin, one is an arbitrary circular motion near the heart that has been assigned to represent our heart attitude but the second is a literal picture of one heading toward a goal—seeking a specific point and then turning away and missing the mark. It shows a turning aside from the intent and purpose of God. Any time I am no longer face to face with the Lord I am probably missing the mark. That is the essence of sin.

It is my deep desire that I know God intimately and follow Him closely. For me, there are days I am right on target and days I feel as if I am not even near the place He wants me in. I take comfort when I read the Bible and see that the people God honored and loved were a lot like me. He took ordinary people and made them outstanding. God was also gracious enough to include their failures and weaknesses so that I could see there is still hope for us mere mortals who wake up late some days and have even gotten out of bed on the wrong side.

I want to have burning passion for my Lord and sometimes I feel Him right next to me and I am doing His will, by the power of His Spirit. Then other times I am just me and I forget that His loving presence is there to get me over the places where I struggle.

If you, like me, want to be right in the center of His will, seeking after His heart, then let's check out some of those hits and misses together.

Aiming for the Heart of God

John 20:29 (KJV) *²⁹ Jesus saith unto him, Thomas, because thou hast seen me, thou hast believed: blessed are they that have not seen, and yet have believed.*

Least Likely to Succeed

Perhaps, like me, you were not voted most likely to succeed. In contrast, neither you nor I were the least likely to succeed. We were all probably part of the faceless masses that go unnoticed and have no claim to fame.

Even when it came to God I wasn't likely to end up saved, much less a minister. I didn't even go to church much as a child. My family had been relatively faithful to a small Presbyterian church until I was five, then their church split and we just never got back to church. By eighteen I was pregnant and unmarried and pretty much a mess. I did not know there was a place in God's heart for losers like me. I was outside of the Christian community.

God had a special relationship with the nation of Israel. They were His people, chosen and loved by the Creator of the universe. If you were outside of that covenant you were not likely to be part of God's story; you were alienated from His blessing, estranged from His family. Most Jews were born into the covenant relationship, but a number of others were led to find covering in that group. There were those who converted to Judaism, proselytes. Much like me, they chose to join the faith.

God had given the Promised Land to the children of Israel. When Joshua arrived at the Jordan, he sent two spies out to survey Jericho. They slipped into the fortified city and entered into a harlot's house near the entrance of the city. They might be able to hear some useful gossip there, and they might not be discovered in a place where men came and left regularly. The woman they found there was more helpful than they expected. When reading the Bible, Rahab was always referred to as a harlot; she was also a Canaanite, born into a family outside of God's covenant people and living a less than virtuous life. Like countless others in Jericho, she had heard of the miracles God had done in Egypt and how He had opened the Red Sea. She risked her life by hiding the spies when the king of Jericho sent for them. This is what she spoke when she had safely diverted the soldiers seeking to kill those two men. **Joshua 2:10-13 (KJV)** *¹⁰ For we have heard how the LORD dried up the water of the Red sea for you, when ye came out of Egypt; and what ye did unto the two kings of the Amorites, that were on the other side Jordan, Sihon and Og, whom ye utterly destroyed. ¹¹ And as soon as we had heard these things, our hearts did melt, neither did there remain any more courage in any man, because of you: for the LORD your God, he is God in heaven above, and in earth beneath. ¹² Now therefore, I pray you, swear unto me by the LORD, since I have shewed you kindness, that ye will also shew kindness unto my father's house, and give me a true token: ¹³ And that ye will save alive my father, and my mother, and my brethren, and my sisters, and all that they have, and deliver our lives from death.* She was choosing to rest in the God of Israel, and trusted His servants to protect her. Those men kept their word, and when the walls of Jericho came tumbling down they sought out and rescued this woman who had shown them kindness and desired refuge with the ones who spoke of her as a dog.

Rahab was putting her trust in a God she had only heard about. She was laying aside her pagan ways and rejecting the idols of her father. "She lived in the midst of a people who were corrupt, abandoned...where vices of the most debasing character were practiced and sanctioned. Rahab was a part of the society about her. However, she was becoming a believer in the one true God." (Beacon p. 30) To be a gentile in a Hebrew setting was nearly as humiliating as being the town harlot had been. She was not accepted with open arms, but was left on the peripheral of the camp. It appears her family later left the multitude of Israelites but Rahab had planted her heart; she would not be deterred. She followed the Hebrews from camp to camp listening to the words of leaders and women milling about doing their chores.

God, who looks at the heart alone, recorded her name in His hall of faith. **Hebrews 11:31 (KJV)**. *³¹ By faith the harlot Rahab perished not with them that believed not, when she had received the spies with peace.* Her faith kept her alive, but it also gave her a future that was greater than her past. Rahab entered into the multitude that traveled with Israel, but most assuredly she put her trust in their God. Salmon was a Jew, one of the two who went in to spy out Jericho. He had hidden in her home. He was a man of honor when she was still a shame-filled nobody who put her trust in the God of Israel. Eventually, her faith impressed him and Salmon married her, and they had a son by the name of Boaz. Rahab's faith had made a place for her when she was outside of the covenant of God. He who sees the heart recognized in her a desire to know Him.

Boaz also married an outsider; Ruth the Moabite. "In a nation that prided itself on being chosen by God and spiritually distinct from others, she was a foreigner from Moab." (Association, p. 372) She chose to follow Naomi back to Israel and trust in the God of Israel. As a widow caring for an aging Mother-in-law, she gleaned the fields of the wealthy Israelite named Boaz. Her compassion and diligence were drawing attention. Boaz watched how she cared for Naomi. When she went into the fields she could have been in danger but both God and Boaz were watching over her. **Ruth 2:8-16 (KJV)** *8 ... Go not to glean in another field, neither go from hence, but abide here fast by my maidens: 9 Let thine eyes be on the field that they do reap, and go thou after them: have I not charged the young men that they shall not touch thee? And when thou art athirst, go unto the vessels, and drink of that which the young men have drawn. 10 Then she fell on her face, and bowed herself to the ground, and said unto him, Why have I found grace in thine eyes, that thou shouldest take knowledge of me, seeing I am a stranger? 11 And Boaz answered and said unto her, It hath fully been shewed me, all that thou hast done unto thy mother in law since the death of thine husband: and how thou hast left thy father and thy mother, and the land of thy nativity, and art come unto a people which thou knewest not heretofore. 12 The LORD recompense thy work, and a full reward be given thee of the LORD God of Israel, under whose wings thou art come to trust. 13 Then she said, Let me find favour in thy sight, my lord; for that thou hast comforted me, and for that thou hast spoken friendly unto thine handmaid, though I be not like unto one* *of thine handmaidens. ¹⁴And Boaz said unto her, At mealtime come thou hither, and eat of the bread, and dip thy morsel in the vinegar. And she sat beside the reapers: and he reached her parched corn, and she did eat, and was sufficed, and left. ¹⁵ And when she was risen up to glean, Boaz commanded his young men, saying, Let her glean even among the sheaves, and reproach her not: ¹⁶And let fall also some of the handfuls of purpose for her, and leave them, that she may glean them, and rebuke her not.*

Maybe because Boaz understood that a foreigner could truly become a part of God's family, he saw her differently than most of the Jews in town. She had found favor and eventually Boaz married Ruth and their first born son was Obed who later had his own son, Jesse. Ruth, a woman with no expectation of acceptance, became a great grandmother to King David. She chose to cling to the God of Israel and He honored her heart. "Boaz is a picture of our Lord Jesus. If you are feeling vulnerable and defenseless right now, imagine Jesus commanding His angels, 'Watch over this one who belongs to Me. Make sure he is treated with respect and not put to shame because he is someone I love and someone whom I died for.' God's Word tells us that if God is for us, none can be against us. [Romans 8:31]" (Prince 9/25/19) Like Rahab and Ruth, we have come under the protection of the Most High. We have been accepted in the beloved and we have a place in the plan of God.

Those women had never known the God of Israel. They did not belong to the covenant people and had not followed their customs. They did not personally see the Red Sea open or any of the other miracles, but they chose to put their trust in the God they had not seen. **John 20:29 (KJV)** *²⁹Jesus saith unto him, Thomas, because thou hast seen me, thou hast believed: blessed are they that have not seen, and yet have believed.* These foreign women did not need to see to believe. Both Rahab and Ruth became part of the linage of Christ. They were unlikely to even be noticed, but God looked beyond their nationality and their upbringing. He looked beyond their spiritual and financial poverty. God did not hold their past against them, but rather He chose to look more than skin deep; He saw into trusting hearts, and He put them in His book of remembrance.

Malachi 3:16-17 (KJV) *¹⁶ Then they that feared the LORD spake often one to another: and the LORD hearkened, and heard it, and a book of remembrance was written before him for them that feared the LORD, and that thought upon his name. ¹⁷ And they shall be mine, saith the LORD of hosts, in that day when I make up my jewels; and I will spare them, as a man spareth his own son that serveth him.* Our Lord is continually looking into the hearts of people. He seeks out those who want Him. He sees past our heritage and our actions, and looks at the intent of the heart. When He finds a heart that will make room for Him, God moves in and places His anointing on the unlikely to succeed and makes them His representatives.

His grace is clearly seen in the lives of Rahab and Ruth and women like me. It was only six weeks after my first baby was born that I married. Just a few months later I went to a revival and gave my whole heart to the God I had just begun to hear about. He took me as I was, and nurtured me into the woman I am today. I thought I was worthless, but God saw something priceless in me.

Isaiah 46:9-10 (KJV) *⁹ ... I am God, and there is none like me, ¹⁰ Declaring the end from the beginning, and from ancient times the things that are not yet done, saying, My counsel shall stand, and I will do all my pleasure:* He took the heart I offered Him. God saw my future potential when I did not have any hope of the life I have now. I have been walking with the Lord for nearly 50 years and He has never once turned away from my sin or failure or weakness, but has always held me close and guided me into His paths. I was nobody, I was not likely to succeed; I was a sinner, a failure with no great prospects, but He put me in His book and got my heart right back on target.

I Samuel 16:7 (KJV) *for the LORD seeth not as man seeth; for man looketh on the outward appearance, but the LORD looketh on the heart.*

Is there anyone else?

If you, like me, were the last one picked to play softball or pretty much any team sport, you understand the shame of being unwanted. I remember team captains looking diligently toward the crowd and then back at me as if they were thinking, "Is there anyone else?"

I am pretty sure that thought went through the mind of those involved in the anointing of Israel's second king. Samuel went by the direction of God to the house of Jesse. God had instructed Samuel to anoint the next king of Israel.

Jesse had eight sons the oldest was Eliab and the youngest was David. Within that family line were those two women who were not eligible for honor in the community much less the linage of Christ. But they were still part of Jesse's family. Rahab and Ruth made it into the list by their faithfulness and good choices. I like to think grandmothers have influence over their little ones. I believe their faith and obedience to God helped mold Jesse, and eventually David into a relationship with the Covenant God of Israel.

We know that fathers in this time diligently passed on the history of Israel to their sons. They spent the most time teaching the law and the covenant to their eldest sons who would one day inherit the bulk of the family wealth and become leader of the tribe. Jesse's grandfather, Boaz, had been rich. So it is likely that Jesse's family was wealthy and respected. Because of their position in the community, and his place in the family, we know that Eliab would have known as much if not more of the stories of Abraham and Noah and all those Old Testament heroes who came before him, than any of his younger brothers. He would have had to memorize genealogy and factual accounts of all the miracles of Exodus. We also know that Eliab had a royal demeanor; he was tall and handsome and strong; so when Samuel came to anoint a king, he took one look at Eliab and knew he was leadership material.

I Samuel 16:6-7 (KJV) *6 And it came to pass, when they were come, that he looked on Eliab, and said, Surely the LORD'S anointed is before him. 7 But the LORD said unto Samuel, Look not on his countenance, or on the height of his stature; because I have refused him: for the LORD seeth not as man seeth; for man looketh on the outward appearance, but the LORD looketh on the heart.* Jesse's seven oldest sons paraded one by one in front of the prophet and none was God's chosen to be king. In despair Samuel asked, "Do you have any other sons? Is there anyone else?" Samuel came under the pretense of a sacrificial feast. They should have included the whole family but they had not sent for David to join them; they totally overlooked David and counted him out. Shepherds were considered unimportant, it was a demanding and unappreciated job, only the poorest and youngest and least of the servants did that job, but David was willingly doing it with diligence and integrity.

I Samuel 16:11-13 (KJV) *11 And Samuel said unto Jesse, Are here all thy children? And he said, There remaineth yet the youngest, and, behold, he keepeth the sheep. And Samuel said unto Jesse, Send and fetch him: for we will not sit down till he come hither. 12 And he sent, and brought him in. Now he was ruddy, and withal of a beautiful countenance, and goodly to look to. And the LORD said, Arise, anoint him: for this is he. 13 Then Samuel took the horn of oil, and anointed him in the midst of his brethren: and the Spirit of the LORD came upon David from that day forward.* They all saw the one they had discounted as God's chosen, at least for that one day. The son that was forgotten was going to be king.

After Saul had been rejected as king, David was anointed to take his place. We know that there were years between that anointing and the time David reigned. Sometime after God took

His hand off of Saul, the first two kings met. **I Samuel 16:14-16 (KJV)** *¹⁴But the Spirit of the LORD departed from Saul, and an evil spirit from the LORD troubled him.* Let's just deal with one thing right here. God did not send or employ any evil spirits. Saul had turned away from God. He was no longer under God's covering. He rejected God's instructions and lost the anointing to lead. Then, the Lord permitted the tormenting spirit to come upon Saul. *¹⁵And Saul's servants said unto him, Behold now, an evil spirit from God troubleth thee. ¹⁶ Let our lord now command thy servants, which are before thee, to seek out a man, who is a cunning player on an harp: and it shall come to pass, when the evil spirit from God is upon thee, that he shall play with his hand, and thou shalt be well.* It was common knowledge then, as it is now, that soothing music can and often will calm an agitated person. More than just peaceful music, David was a psalmist who wrote a good number of worship songs. His songs welcomed the Spirit of God and where the presence of the Lord is, peace follows. So they sought out a man skilled in worship and brought him to the worrisome king. **I Samuel 16:21-23 (KJV)** *²¹ And David came to Saul, and stood before him: and he loved him greatly; and he became his armorbearer. ²² And Saul sent to Jesse, saying, Let David, I pray thee, stand before me; for he hath found favour in my sight. ²³ And it came to pass, when the evil spirit from God was upon Saul, that David took an harp, and played with his hand: so Saul was refreshed, and was well, and the evil spirit departed from him.* David must not have stayed there continually, perhaps after Saul improved he was sent home.

Fast forward some years, we don't really know how many but now Israel is at war with the Philistines and Eliab and the next two sons were called into military service. The other five sons are too young or exempt because their older brothers are fulfilling the family obligation.

I Samuel 17:3-11 (KJV) *³ And the Philistines stood on a mountain on the one side, and Israel stood on a mountain on the other side: and there was a valley between them. ⁴ And there went out a champion out of the camp of the Philistines, named Goliath,* *of Gath, whose height was six cubits and a span. ⁵ And he had an helmet of brass upon his head, and he was armed with a coat of mail; and the weight of the coat was five thousand shekels of brass. ⁶ And he had greaves of brass upon his legs, and a target of brass between his shoulders. ⁷ And the staff of his spear was like a weaver's beam; and his spear's head weighed six hundred shekels of iron: and one bearing a shield went before him.* That enemy soldier is nine feet nine inches tall, all muscle, heavily armed, and covered by some serious armor. *⁸ And he stood and cried unto the armies of Israel, and said unto them, Why are ye come out to set your battle in array? Am not I a Philistine, and ye servants to Saul? Choose you a man for you, and let him come down to me. ⁹ If he be able to fight with me, and to kill me, then will we be your servants: but if I prevail against him, and kill him, then shall ye be our servants, and serve us. ¹⁰ And the Philistine said, I defy the armies of Israel this day; give me a man, that we may fight together. ¹¹ When Saul and all Israel heard those words of the Philistine, they were dismayed, and greatly afraid.* That man mocked them, and made light of their strength and their God. They feared because looking in the natural they were already defeated and would either be killed or enslaved.

By all rights Saul should have gone down against Goliath, he was king, he was a full head taller than all the other men, but he was hiding in his tent when along comes David. When David hears what Goliath shouted and sees their reaction, he was moved with righteous anger. He was not there to fight, he was there to supply the warriors and check for word on his brothers. He did more than that; he listened to this heathen insulting the nation and God who kept them. Holy indignation and boldness rose up in David. That same spirit of excellence, and that same trusting heart are still in the shepherd/king when he sees the conflict. **I Samuel 17:26-29 (KJV)** *²⁶ And David spake to the men that stood by him, saying, What shall be done to the man that killeth this Philistine, and taketh away the reproach from Israel? For who is this uncircumcised Philistine, that he should defy the armies of the living God?* That man doesn't even know God, we have a covenant with God, and we can't lose. Those are the words of a man who has spent time with the Lord. David knows who he trusts in. He has worshiped and followed the God of Israel so he is unafraid. *²⁸ And Eliab his eldest brother heard when he spake unto the men; and Eliab's anger was kindled against David, and he said, Why camest thou down hither? and with whom hast thou left those few sheep in the wilderness? I know thy pride, and the naughtiness of thine heart; for thou art come down that thou mightest see the battle. ²⁹ And David said, What have I now done? Is there not a cause?* Why is Eliab being such a jerk to his brother? I think it is because he knew David would rise up and volunteer to take on the giant. Eliab is the eldest son; if one of the sons of Jesse is to fight it should be him. Eliab is thinking not me, don't make me look bad, don't make me feel like I should fight, just go on back to dad and work in the fields and keep out of it. David already got promoted right in front of him once and he isn't eager to see this kid show him up again. That fear and jealousy ruled Eliab. It is the heart that God saw in Eliab that disqualified him.

God also saw the difference in the heart of David that made him the next king. **I Samuel 17:31-32 (KJV)** *³¹ And when the words were heard which David spake, they rehearsed them before Saul: and he sent for him. ³² And David said to Saul, Let no man's heart fail because of him; thy servant will go and fight with this Philistine.* David said I will go and fight. When he is brought to Saul, he is unrecognized. If the king and the army are afraid, send in the shepherd boy. Send in someone who has already built a relationship with the God who can never fail.

I Samuel 17:33-37 (KJV) *³³ And Saul said to David, Thou art not able to go against this Philistine to fight with him: for thou art but a youth, and he a man of war from his youth.* You are too young and inexperienced. *³⁴ And David said unto Saul, Thy servant kept his father's sheep, and there came a lion, and a bear, and took a lamb out of the flock: ³⁵ And I went out after him, and smote him, and delivered it out of his mouth: and when he arose against me, I caught him by his beard, and smote him, and slew him. ³⁶ Thy servant slew both the lion and the bear: and this uncircumcised Philistine shall be as one of them, seeing he hath defied the armies* *of the living God.* *³⁷ David said moreover, The LORD that delivered me out of the paw of the lion, and out of the paw of the bear, he will deliver me out of the hand of this Philistine.* He rehearsed his past victories and recognized the covenant he had with God and that got him in position to win. His heart and attitude were right on target. *And Saul said unto David, Go, and the LORD be with thee.* Even an outsider can see that relationship with God makes men powerful and successful. The anointing which was once on Saul is resting upon David and even the most spiritually bankrupt can see the presence of God on those who bear the calling and anointing.

I Samuel 17:40 (KJV) *⁴⁰ And he took his staff in his hand, and chose him five smooth stones out of the brook, and put them in a shepherd's bag which he had, even in a scrip; and his sling was in his hand: and he drew near to the Philistine.* Armed as he was in the fields, David walked out onto the battlefield knowing that God walked every step with him. His trust in God made him bold.

I Samuel 17:45-51 (KJV) *⁴⁵ Then said David to the Philistine, Thou comest to me with a sword, and with a spear, and with a shield: but I come to thee in the name of the LORD of hosts, the God of the armies of Israel, whom thou hast defied. ⁴⁶ This day will the LORD deliver thee into mine hand; and I will smite thee, and take thine head from thee; and I will give the carcases of the host of the Philistines this day unto the fowls of the air, and to the wild beasts of the earth; that all the earth may know that there is a God in Israel. ⁴⁷ And all this assembly shall know that the LORD saveth not with sword and spear: for the battle is the LORD'S, and he will give you into our hands.* That is confidence speaking. Not self-confidence, but an assurance based on faith in God alone. David is not standing there alone; he is walking in the shadow of the Almighty. *⁴⁸ And it came to pass, when the Philistine arose, and came and drew nigh to meet David, that David hasted, and ran toward the army to meet the Philistine.* Not today devil, I will not fear; I will fight. I am running to the battle. I am covered by the covenant blood of the lamb. I am more than a conqueror through the One who loves me. *⁴⁹ And David put his hand in his bag, and* *took thence a stone, and slang it, and smote the Philistine in his forehead, that the stone sunk into his forehead; and he fell upon his face to the earth. [50] So David prevailed over the Philistine with a sling and with a stone, and smote the Philistine, and slew him; but there was no sword in the hand of David. [51] Therefore David ran, and stood upon the Philistine, and took his sword, and drew it out of the sheath thereof, and slew him, and cut off his head therewith. And when the Philistines saw their champion was dead, they fled.*

There was something real in the heart of David that attracted God. This man who was overlooked by his family, walked in greatness and failure. He was later caught in an adulterous relationship, sometimes angry and vengeful, and a man of war, but he was also precious to God. David would fail sometimes, but he always repented and he chose to honor God; he leaned hard on his relationship with God. More than anything else, David loved the Lord. **Acts 13:22 (KJV)** ... *He raised up unto them David to be their king; to whom also he gave testimony, and said, I have found David the son of Jesse, a man after mine own heart, which shall fulfil all my will.* David was far from perfect, but he had it in his heart to worship and to serve the God of Israel. It is always about the heart. That was the same heart that got Rahab and Ruth into the linage of Christ. It is what got the unlikely to succeed into places of honor all throughout time.

Now what about us? You and I have times of greatness and times of failure too. I have found that when I am less than my best and my aim for the heart of God seems a little off that I need to follow the example of David. I worship my way back on target. It is often hard to pray when you feel disconnected from the Lord. I remember once when I was struggling to feel close to God and He spoke to my heart. "Just stay in my presence a little longer and stay in my favor and grace, stay within my spirit and receive of me. Stay and I will fill you up and make you whole. Stay and I will satisfy that longing in your soul. Come to me and love on me until your heart overflows with my love for you." Worship breaks barriers that nothing else will.

There is an example that I remember Brother Kenneth Hagin sharing at one of his conferences years ago. He said as a young evangelist he was staying in the home of a pastor. A church member was very ill and near death so the pastor and his wife went to the home of their parishioner to pray. The young evangelist was asked to accompany them. When they arrived they found the man was in horrible convulsions. Those gathered around the bedside prayed earnestly. The pastor spoke with great authority and yet there was no change. Then quietly the pastor's wife began to sing. Just a simple worship chorus in a small voice but something started to happen. Others in the room added their voices to her song of praise and the convulsions stopped the man seemed to improve. When they stopped singing the man returned to his former state and again they all cried out in prayer and again nothing happened. This time when she started to sing they understood and each man present took up the worship that had such an effect on the atmosphere. This time the man rose up completely whole. Prayer matters and fighting in prayer is valid, but there is something incredibly powerful in worship.

I have never forgotten that when all is dark and the struggle is hard, worship will work. I asked God once about my own prayer and praise life. He said the best worship I ever gave Him was not when I sang a solo at church, or preached or taught a class. It was not when I wept in His presence or danced in the Spirit. My best praise did not come during any formal worship or even at the church. He said I gave my best offering of praise in an ICU room where my 12 year old daughter lay in a coma, as I softly sang a short chorus about standing on Jesus, the rock of my salvation. That song did not feel anointed, or sound especially good. It felt like I was struggling to breathe. The medical staff had never said one word of encouragement that would cause me to sing; the prognosis was horrible. The doctors gave us no hope, but God was still my God. He was still worthy of praise and if my daughter survived it would be all Him. As hard as it is to say, even if she died or was left in a state of brain damage that would have been worse than death, He was still worthy of praise. In my heart I was saying that I would love and serve my Lord regardless of the outcome. That stand and my tiny solo voice in the darkest moment of my life was worship that God honored. In my heart, that worship broke the hold of death off of my little girl. It also established an immovable foundation in my prayer life. I tend to worship more than I ask and it always brings me back on target.

Ephesians 2:10 (KJV) *¹⁰ For we are his workmanship, created in Christ Jesus unto good works, which God hath before ordained that we should walk in them.*

Judas or Peter Endings

Of all the Disciples of Christ, the one with the most promise and business sense was Judas. He could have been great but he became a thief and he betrayed our Lord. His heart wasn't right. **Matthew 26:23-25 (KJV)** *²³ And he answered and said, He that dippeth his hand with me in the dish, the same shall betray me. ²⁴ The Son of man goeth as it is written of him: but woe unto that man by whom the Son of man is betrayed! it had been good for that man if he had not been born.²⁵ Then Judas, which betrayed him, answered and said, Master, is it I? He said unto him, Thou hast said.* We know that Judas did betray the Lord; he sold out the Messiah for a handful of cash, and when he was mindful of the cost he wanted to undo it. **Matthew 27:2-5 (KJV)** *² And when they had bound him, they led him away, and delivered him to Pontius Pilate the governor. ³ Then Judas, which had betrayed him, when he saw that he was condemned, repented himself, and brought again the thirty pieces of silver to the chief priests and elders, ⁴ Saying, I have sinned in that I have betrayed the innocent blood. And they said, What is that to us? see thou to that. ⁵ And he cast down the pieces of silver in the temple, and departed, and went and hanged himself.* Judas never recovered from his failure; he killed himself. Even if he sincerely repented and was totally forgiven, he locked himself into a place of failure that never showed on earth. How sad that he made his greatest mistake his legacy.

Another man betrayed Jesus at the same time. That man was Peter. **Mark 14:66-72 (KJV)** *⁶⁶ And as Peter was beneath in the palace, there cometh one of the maids of the high priest: ⁶⁷ And when she saw Peter warming himself, she looked upon him, and said, And thou also wast with Jesus of Nazareth. ⁶⁸ But he denied, saying, I know not, neither understand I what thou sayest. And he went out into the porch; and the cock crew. ⁶⁹ And a maid saw him* *again, and began to say to them that stood by, This is one of them.* ⁷⁰ *And he denied it again. And a little after, they that stood by said again to Peter, Surely thou art one of them: for thou art a Galilaean, and thy speech agreeth thereto.* ⁷¹ *But he began to curse and to swear, saying, I know not this man of whom ye speak.* ⁷² *And the second time the cock crew. And Peter called to mind the word that Jesus said unto him, Before the cock crow twice, thou shalt deny me thrice. And when he thought thereon, he wept.*

Peter's heart was crushed by his moral failure; when he denied Jesus, it could have been the end for him too. The heart of Peter led him to real repentance and service. Peter could have stayed a failure but God saw in his heart a leader of the faith.

God did two things that motivated Peter to walk out his calling. First he made sure Peter knew he wasn't outside of grace. The angel at the tomb gave him a message through Mary. **Mark 16:7 (KJV)** ⁷ *But go your way, tell his disciples and Peter that he goeth before you into Galilee: there shall ye see him, as he said unto you.* Make sure you tell Peter. He made sure that Peter knew he was still welcome and part of the fold. Then when Jesus appeared to them by the Sea, He led Peter into healing repentance and renewed his call.

John 21:15-19 (KJV) ¹⁵ *So when they had dined, Jesus saith to Simon Peter, Simon, son of Jonas, lovest thou me more than these? He saith unto him, Yea, Lord; thou knowest that I love thee. He saith unto him, Feed my lambs.* ¹⁶ *He saith to him again the second time, Simon, son of Jonas, lovest thou me? He saith unto him, Yea, Lord; thou knowest that I love thee. He saith unto him, Feed my sheep.* ¹⁷ *He saith unto him the third time, Simon, son of Jonas, lovest thou me? Peter was grieved because he said unto him the third time, Lovest thou me? And he said unto him, Lord, thou knowest all things; thou knowest that I love thee. Jesus saith unto him, Feed my sheep.* ¹⁸ *Verily, verily, I say unto thee, When thou wast young, thou girdedst thyself, and walkedst whither thou wouldest: but when thou shalt be old, thou shalt stretch forth thy hands, and another shall gird thee, and carry thee whither thou* *wouldest not.* ⁱ⁹ *This spake he, signifying by what death he should glorify God. And when he had spoken this, he saith unto him, Follow me.* Peter got to say I love you three times. Once for every word of denial, he was allowed to commit to love and service. After he had recognized that the past could not hold him captive, Peter was ready for the rest of the message. The Lord told him that he would die for his faith just as he feared when he first said I do not know Him. Now that he knows the power of the resurrected Christ; he will never yield to fear again, and he will follow knowing the cost. Peter spent the rest of his life proclaiming the One he had denied.

These are a few of the words Peter spoke when powerful men confronted him. **Acts 4:10-13 (KJV)** ¹⁰ *Be it known unto you all, and to all the people of Israel, that by the name of Jesus Christ of Nazareth, whom ye crucified, whom God raised from the dead, even by him doth this man stand here before you whole.* ¹¹ *This is the stone which was set at nought of you builders, which is become the head of the corner.* ¹² *Neither is there salvation in any other: for there is none other name under heaven given among men, whereby we must be saved.* ¹³ *Now when they saw the boldness of Peter and John, and perceived that they were unlearned and ignorant men, they Marveled; and they took knowledge of them, that they had been with Jesus.* Peter was a changed man who had decided to follow regardless of cost. They saw that his relationship with Jesus made him a bold man of faith. Isn't that what we all want? Our life, our testimony should be so in tune with the heart of God that our words, our actions, our countenance says we have been with Jesus and that He alone is our focus.

There was one other man who had a choice to believe or doubt that I wanted to mention. That would be Thomas. When the resurrected Lord appeared to His disciples they were overjoyed. But not everyone was quick to believe. **John 20:24-29 (KJV)** ²⁴ *But Thomas, one of the twelve, called Didymus, was not with them when Jesus came.* ²⁵ *The other disciples therefore said unto him, We have seen the Lord. But he said unto them, Except I shall see in his hands the print of the nails, and put my finger into the print of the* *nails, and thrust my hand into his side, I will not believe.* ²⁶ *And after eight days again his disciples were within, and Thomas with them: then came Jesus, the doors being shut, and stood in the midst, and said, Peace be unto you.* ²⁷ *Then saith he to Thomas, Reach hither thy finger, and behold my hands; and reach hither thy hand, and thrust it into my side: and be not faithless, but believing.* ²⁸ *And Thomas answered and said unto him, My Lord and my God.* ²⁹ *Jesus saith unto him, Thomas, because thou hast seen me, thou hast believed: blessed are they that have not seen, and yet have believed.* If the Lord had not appeared a second time when Thomas was there, his testimony would have been hearsay. He refused to really believe without first hand experiential knowledge of the resurrection. The ministry assigned to Thomas almost never happened. I find it fascinating that the same man who said I will not believe unless I see was also the first to fall down on his knees and declare that Jesus was indeed God. It was vital that Thomas believe. Every disciple that testified of the resurrection did it at the threat of death. He had to know that his faith was anchored in truth.

Some of us are like Thomas, for a time we question or deny or doubt, but given a chance we will turn to Christ. My husband had a season when he served the historical Jesus, rather than the Redeemer he walks with now. God makes it so easy for us to turn to Him afresh.

Just like Thomas, God gave Peter time to get it right, to repent and make his life count. Peter wrote this several years later so that we would know that God is allowing others time to get back on track as well. **II Peter 3:9 (KJV)** ⁹ *The Lord is not slack concerning his promise, as some men count slackness; but is longsuffering to us-ward, not willing that any should perish, but that all should come to repentance.* We don't have to make our failures our legacy like Judas. We can pick ourselves back up and start over at any time. We can take another look at the cross and the empty tomb and know that Christ has made a way of escape from our past failures. Like Peter we can allow the failures of our past to be just a memory, a moment in time, and not the place where we live.

John Newton was a British captain who owned his own slave ship. He was known to be a harsh, cruel man towards his crew and the poor souls that he carried as cargo to be sold into slavery. That is a lot of baggage to carry around. One night in the midst of a really bad storm at sea, John came to himself. He cried out to God for help and forgiveness. It was that same man, John Newton, who wrote Amazing Grace. His legacy is one of the most sung hymns of all time. He was a cruel slaver, but by grace he met a Savior who called him into the ministry. That man who could have died a failure and a sinner, hated by many, became a pastor who led many to the Lord. God mercifully changed his destiny.

Ephesians 2:10 (KJV) *¹⁰ For we are his workmanship, created in Christ Jesus unto good works, which God hath before ordained that we should walk in them.* We are still under construction. Our destiny is better than our worst mistake or our moments of doubt. He has allowed us a moment of revelation and some amazing grace. He has assured us an eternal future in Christ. We can move closer, and see clearer, and be more than we are today. To every Judas and Peter and Thomas among us He would say, "Never let a failure define you. You aren't finished yet." If you have missed the mark, get your eyes back on the target and take hold of the bow and arrow in your hands. Start afresh, aim well and let nothing get between you and your designated target.

I Timothy 1:15 (KJV) *¹⁵ This is a faithful saying, and worthy of all acceptation, that Christ Jesus came into the world to save sinners; of whom I am chief.*

Zealous Servants

When Saul of Tarsus was jailing and killing Christians, it wasn't because he was evil by nature, it was because he was zealous as a Jew. He thought he was protecting the Hebrew way of life from being threatened. He excelled in every area, he was sincere in his faith, but he was sincerely wrong. His hatred for Christians was rooted in religion. He was trying to work hard to live as a Jew that excelled in knowledge and in service. When he describes his life before he was saved, he says this. **Philippians 3:4-6 (KJV)** *4 Though I might also have confidence in the flesh. If any other man thinketh that he hath whereof he might trust in the flesh, I more: 5 Circumcised the eighth day, of the stock of Israel, of the tribe of Benjamin, an Hebrew of the Hebrews; as touching the law, a Pharisee; 6 Concerning zeal, persecuting the church; touching the righteousness which is in the law, blameless.* Saul [later called Paul] was full of self-assurance and self-righteousness; all that fleshly effort did nothing for him. He was rich, well educated, both a Hebrew and a Roman citizen. He was respected within his community. He was a powerful man. He was also lost. Then he found Christ and turned it all around.

Philippians 3:7-14 *7 But what things were gain to me, those I counted loss for Christ. 8 Yea doubtless, and I count all things but loss for the excellency of the knowledge of Christ Jesus my Lord: for whom I have suffered the loss of all things, and do count them but dung, that I may win Christ, 9 And be found in him, not having mine own righteousness, which is of the law, but that which is through the faith of Christ, the righteousness which is of God by faith: 10 That I may know him, and the power of his resurrection, and the fellowship of his sufferings, being made conformable unto his death; 11 If by any means I might attain unto* *the resurrection of the dead. ¹²Not as though I had already attained, either were already perfect: but I follow after, if that I may apprehend that for which also I am apprehended of Christ Jesus. ¹³Brethren, I count not myself to have apprehended: but this one thing I do, forgetting those things which are behind, and reaching forth unto those things which are before, ¹⁴I press toward the mark for the prize of the high calling of God in Christ Jesus.*

Saul was running full speed ahead in the wrong direction. God was able to turn him from the terror and enemy of every Christian into a faithful believer who preached the gospel. Paul was constantly arrested and beaten for the faith he had tried to snuff out. Sometimes I wonder if he felt like he was reaping what he sowed. We know he sang midnight praises to God in prison. His relationship was so strong that God answered his worship with an earthquake and a revival. [Acts 16] Paul did not get to see the miracles of Jesus. He was not there to hear the Lord teach the masses. He most likely did not see the crucifixion or the empty tomb. He did not see the resurrected Christ, or see Jesus ascend into heaven. He was not there on the day of Pentecost. Every other disciple that turned apostle had more first-hand experience than Paul. He was more like us, than any of those men who I have envied for their time with the Lord. I always thought how wonderful it would have been to experience those things they saw and heard. God didn't call Paul in time to see and hear all of that, if He had, Paul would not have been killing Christians. God let him come to Christ later. He came by faith. Paul could have been like Thomas who refused to believe Jesus was alive even after seeing so many miracles. For Thomas the sight of Jesus dead on the cross was final. Paul did not have to see a resurrected Christ to believe. Perhaps, that was so we could see the drastic change that was possible when men like him are saved. God let the converted Paul influence and inspire so many lost souls. God also called him to pen more than two thirds of the New Testament. If the heart wants to be right, God can change the direction.

Paul saw his past through the blood and recognized that his zeal had cost the lives of other believers. He had been so wrong but he realized that through his failures and past sin God could show others that there is hope for anyone. He wrote as much in his letter to Timothy. **I Timothy 1:12-16 (KJV)** *12 And I thank Christ Jesus our Lord, who hath enabled me, for that he counted me faithful, putting me into the ministry; 13 Who was before a blasphemer, and a persecutor, and injurious: but I obtained mercy, because I did it ignorantly in unbelief. 14 And the grace of our Lord was exceeding abundant with faith and love which is in Christ Jesus. 15 This is a faithful saying, and worthy of all acceptation, that Christ Jesus came into the world to save sinners; of whom I am chief. 16 Howbeit for this cause I obtained mercy, that in me first Jesus Christ might shew forth all longsuffering, for a pattern to them which should hereafter believe on him to life everlasting.* Paul became one of God's greatest spokesmen, a faithful and still zealous servant.

Speaking of servants, remember Gehazi, servant to Elisha? He was one on one with the prophet day and night for several years. He served Elisha as Elisha had served Elijah. He could have taken on a double portion of his master's anointing, but instead his heart betrayed him and he became a selfish man who chose money over the anointing and ended up a leper. [II Kings 5]

We have something to say about our destiny. We choose the level of heart commitment we have to our Lord. Everyone is as close to God as they decide to be. You would not be reading this if you didn't have a heart like David and Peter and Paul. Rahab and Ruth didn't have a chance to walk out their faith until they chose God over their own lives and their own people and made an opening for their future. Don't you see that we were all nobodies? Most of us were not wealthy, or mighty, or came from the right family like Saul of Tarsus. We all came by simply accepting the grace that was offered to us.

I have been told I am stubborn. I prefer the word steadfast, but ok I don't back down very easily on what I believe. I will defend my cause and fight for truth. I was just as lost as Paul and have often wavered along the way, but I know in whom I have believed. I know God is faithful; so now my cause, my strong foundation, is Christ. I wish that men everywhere would come to know and to trust in Him. I teach and preach what I know in order to draw men closer. Have I ever missed the mark? I have. There were times I did not speak up and times that my message was unclear. There were times I was not a very good example of what a servant of Christ should really be. At times, I got too far away from my Lord and could not see the target at all. But by the same grace God offered to Paul I am standing today.

Aiming for the Heart of God

Hebrews 11:1-2 (KJV) [1] *Now faith is the substance of things hoped for, the evidence of things not seen.* [2] *For by it the elders obtained a good report.*

God's Next Hall of Faith

I recommend that you read the whole eleventh chapter of Hebrews, where God acknowledged men and women of faith. **Hebrews 11:1-2 (KJV)** *1 Now faith is the substance of things hoped for, the evidence of things not seen. 2 For by it the elders obtained a good report.* There is this long list of our Bible heroes who by faith did one great thing after another. I know it is hard sometimes to think of those people as just like us. I understand that sometimes what we do seems small and yet somehow I believe that God still looks at the heart and allows us to be part of His story. I want us to live in such a way that we could be listed in the books of heaven as faithful and obedient and anointed.

I wonder what it would take to be in the next hall of faith. Really everyone who is listed in the current one simply received something miraculous from the Lord. Yes they believed, and yes they held on to the promises, but it was really God who did the great works. All it really says is by faith these people received or acted in obedience. Maybe we could do just that. We might never fight a giant or build an ark, but believe God and just obey—we have a shot at that.

Maybe we didn't make it into the Hall of faith that first time but look what it says in Malachi. **Malachi 3:16-17 (KJV)** *16 Then they that feared the LORD spake often one to another: and the LORD hearkened, and heard it, and a book of remembrance was written before him for them that feared the LORD, and that thought upon his name. 17 And they shall be mine, saith the LORD of hosts, in that day when I make up my jewels; and I will spare them, as a man spareth his own son that serveth him.* Maybe men and women like us are still recorded as faithful and obedient servants who received by faith.

Rev. Kathryn L. Smith

I would like to share a little of Joseph's story with you. Just maybe you can imagine it in the books of heaven; I can. Joseph is a young man about twenty. He comes to church some, but not all the time. His dad, Dean, comes faithfully. About three weeks ago Joseph was working under his Jeep and the car fell on him. It was still running and the rear passenger tire was directly on his chest and spinning. That is over a ton of weight directly on his rib cage. The driver side tire was spinning too. In fact the driver's side tire dug a hole in the pavement and wore the tread down to the metal rim, before they got it stopped and off of him.

God did some miraculous things for him, none of which Joseph remembers. Several people saw the car fall and called 911. A neighbor ran out of her house and held his limp hand praying until help arrived. A tow truck was on that street and got canceled just in time to get the emergency call for help. The driver was able to lift the car off of him, but Joseph was not breathing. His face was a deep eggplant purple. The first responders got him hooked to a ventilator, but he was probably without air for about 15-20 minutes. That is a very long time. Brain damage normally occurs after as little as five minutes without oxygen.

They airlifted him to one of the larger area hospitals. His prognosis was not good. They knew he had five broken ribs and a punctured lung and really did not worry about much else because they did not expect him to survive transport let alone make it through the day.

When Dean got word of his son's accident, he said something rose up in him. It was sort of a determination that caused him to say over and over "Devil you won't take my boy. You can't have my son." When Dean got to see him, he did not even recognize his son. Joseph was purple, swollen and connected to tubes and wires. The only movement Dean saw was the gentle rise and fall of forced air going into his body from the respirator. The medical staff kept looking at his eyes and Dean heard them say no response. For hours they checked Joseph for any pupil dilation when they shined light into his eyes. No change, no response.

They were really looking for signs of brain activity and there was none. For all intents and purposes Joseph was dead. Something in Dean could not really grasp that his son was dead. He just knew that they kept saying no response.

It was several hours before our Pastor went into the room. Family had come and gone with no improvement, no real hope. When Pastor Tim prayed a very simple prayer, he said something about staying strong or fighting. Suddenly, Joe started to move, his feet and hands jerked, and then he tried to sit up in the bed. His eyes were still closed but he had moved. When Dean took his hand and asked a question, Joe was able to respond by squeezing his hand. They now knew there was a live Joseph in that seriously bruised body. There were still a lot of concerns, but from that moment on there was hope. God had begun to do what no doctor could. He was about to show all of them the miraculous power that comes from believing God.

The doctors slowly reduced his medication and when the swelling in his brain subsided some they began to consider that he might recover. In just another day or so, they tried to remove the oxygen, but his body didn't respond by breathing unaided. They waited a while longer and when they tried again, he was able to breathe on his own. When they pulled the tubing from his throat he asked about his jeep. That was a very normal Joseph.

There were small victories along the way, bits of improvement that those of us on the prayer chain rejoiced over. Just a few days later Joseph was out of bed and the normal color had returned to his face. Dean walked with him to the cafeteria where the Chaplain, who had been there when Joseph arrived, happened to walk past them. He stopped to ask Dean about his son. Dean smiled and said, "This is the miracle man right here." That chaplain was shocked. He knew there was pretty much nothing anyone could do for the young man he had seen a few days earlier. He did not even recognize Joseph as the same person. He was overwhelmed with joy and thankful for what only God could have done.

Joseph came to church the next week and to my house on Christmas Eve and he seems perfect. We found out that he also severed a ligament connecting his shoulder to his collar bone but even that seems to be healing at an accelerated rate. The doctors say they won't even need to do surgery on it.

Hebrews 11:1 (KJV) *¹Now faith is the substance of things hoped for, the evidence of things not seen.* By faith, Dean and all of Joseph's family and friends obtained a miracle; he that was dead was restored to life. Dean said he always thought it was amazing to hear about the ones who received a miracle, but now that he has experienced one, he knows the agony and struggle that goes with that miracle. He never wants to need another one.

I get it. I have been that parent. It is the worst thing ever to watch your child lay in the ICU while doctors try to prepare you for their death or maybe worse yet to say that they lived and are brain damaged and will forever need to be cared for as if they were a baby. I know that for me, standing in faith was the only choice I had. Dean did basically the same thing I did. He stood against the devil and trusted in God. **James 4:7 (KJV)** *⁷Submit yourselves therefore to God. Resist the devil, and he will flee from you.* Dean knew in his heart that a loving God heard and cared and he trusted that the blood of Jesus was enough for even this impossible looking situation. He determined that Christ could heal his son and even if that was not the case, he would still believe.

Our church has been emphasizing this scripture throughout the past year. **I John 5:14-15 (KJV)** *¹⁴And this is the confidence that we have in him, that, if we ask any thing according to his will, he heareth us: ¹⁵And if we know that he hear us, whatsoever we ask, we know that we have the petitions that we desired of him.* Having asked and seen the results we can declare that the Lord really does hear and answer prayer.

Hebrews 12:1-3 (KJV) *¹Wherefore seeing we also are compassed about with so great a cloud of witnesses, let us lay aside every weight, and the sin which doth so easily beset us, and* *let us run with patience the race that is set before us,* ² *Looking unto Jesus the author and finisher of our faith; who for the joy that was set before him endured the cross, despising the shame, and is set down at the right hand of the throne of God.* ³ *For consider him that endured such contradiction of sinners against himself, lest ye be wearied and faint in your minds.*

Consider those who overcame, those who asked and believed and received something from God. Maybe not just the witnesses in the Bible, but also those that we have all around us today, consider them and hold tightly to your faith. Men like Dean, who received a miracle, can encourage us in our time of need. Not everyone gets the results that Dean did, or I did. Some ask and pray and face deep loss and disappointment. That does not mean their faith is defective, but according to Deuteronomy 29:29 the secret things belong to the Lord. We do not have all the answers, even those men and women in the Hebrews 11 hall of faith did not receive everything they believed for in their lifetime. But God honors the ones who face adversity and still believe. When we trust God against all odds we are right on target.

Luke 19:10 (KJV) *¹⁰ For the Son of man is come to seek and to save that which was lost.*

His Goodness is running after me

When Jesus told a story He had reason to believe that it would be helpful to those in the immediate crowd and to us. One of the best known parables is that of the prodigal son. I think that most of us relate to this story pretty well. **Luke 15:11-12 (KJV)** *11 And he said, A certain man had two sons: 12 And the younger of them said to his father, Father, give me the portion of goods that falleth to me. And he divided unto them his living.* The boy pretty much said, "I wish you were dead; I don't want to follow your rules or work for your benefit. I don't need you and I don't want you but I want what you have." That is heart wrenching for me as a parent. This father loved his sons so much that he gave them the freedom to do what they wished. He granted his younger son's request.

In a Jewish home the older son was given twice the inheritance of the father's wealth. So we know that the younger son asked the man for one third of his estate. During that time the man probably had most of his wealth tied up in animals and land. He probably had to sell things in order to give this rebellious son the inheritance he demanded. Assuming that is so, he not only insulted his father, but publicly put him to shame. In spite of all of that, we never hear the father rebuke his son.

Most of us do not realize that the older son had special responsibilities. Among those, it was his job to be the peace keeper. He should have intervened between his younger brother and his dad. It was his job to shut down such an offensive demand within the family. He could have done a number of things to stop his brother from leaving but he did nothing.

Luke 15:13-16 (KJV) *¹³ And not many days after the younger son gathered all together, and took his journey into a far country, and there wasted his substance with riotous living.* He was out from under the control of his father, and he thinks it's time to party. Every drunk is popular when he is buying a round for the house. This kid has lots of short term friends to eat and drink and carouse with as long as he is buying. He is living a life that is very different from that which he had at home. He seems to have neglected to pack any moral compass when he was leaving. All indications are that he is living a rather sinful life while he is running from responsibility and all he has been taught. He is in a state of full rebellion. *¹⁴ And when he had spent all, there arose a mighty famine in that land; and he began to be in want.* That is the trouble with money that you did not work for and took lightly it spends quickly and then it is just gone. Here he is in a foreign land and all his party hardy buddies are gone. He has no income and soon no one will extend him credit. He becomes poor and desperate. *¹⁵ And he went and joined himself to a citizen of that country; and he sent him into his fields to feed swine. ¹⁶ And he would fain have filled his belly with the husks that the swine did eat: and no man gave unto him.* The pigs ate carob pods and even if he tried to eat those they were not filling and could not be fully digested. This man who was a Hebrew would have never touched any unclean animal before this. The Jews did not eat pork, most did not raise hogs but if they did raise them for the gentiles around them to buy, only the poorest and lowliest slaves would have fed them. Our previously prosperous young man has sunk so low that he is in the muck with the pigs and thinks they have it better than he does. He has reached the bottom of the pit.

Luke 15:17-20 (KJV) *¹⁷ And when he came to himself, he said, How many hired servants of my father's have bread enough and to spare, and I perish with hunger! ¹⁸ I will arise and go to my father, and will say unto him, Father, I have sinned against heaven, and before thee, ¹⁹ And am no more worthy to be called thy son: make me as one of thy hired servants. ²⁰ And he arose, and came to his father.* He had refused to work as a son and now he is willing to beg to be treated as a hired hand. He knows he has severed ties with his father, but he hopes he can at least get a job from the father that he now sees as a good man.

Our prodigal sets off to go back home. Remember that when he left home he had money to maybe ride a donkey or camel, but now he is walking the great distance. When he left home he could stay in an inn when he was tired, but now he is sleeping in ditches and rocky places, wherever he can. He is tired and hungry and dirty and in danger every step of the way. There are thieves and murderers in the shadows. He has nothing to offer them to spare his life. His feet are tired, and shame has weighed him down. His sin doesn't set well with him now. It is a long trip and I am sure he rehearsed that speech asking for mercy from a father he had insulted and rejected. In his mind, I am sure he thinks he has maybe a small chance at a job and a roof over his head. He sees long days of hard work ahead but that is so much better than the life he has now. The life of sin has left him spiritually and emotionally bankrupt. He has lost more than his money and pride.

Meanwhile, back at the ranch, his father has mourned the loss of his son. I think he has prayed for his safety and his return. Many days this man has gone outside and looked down the road in hopes of seeing his son. **Luke 15:21 (KJV)** *But when he was yet a great way off, his father saw him, and had compassion, and ran, and fell on his neck, and kissed him.* Fathers did not run, they stood and waited. But this man's heart was so moved that he could not wait any longer; his compassion set his feet in motion. "Though it was improper in Jewish culture, the father held up his robe and ran... The father was in a hurry because he had seen his son, who was still a long way from home. He was running toward his son as he could not wait to embrace and kiss his child again." (Prince 11/2/19) His love drove him to lay aside all dignity and social status to get to the son he loved. The Amplified Bible says *the father was moved with pity and tenderness and ran embracing him fervently!* *²¹ And the son said unto him, Father, I have sinned against heaven, and in thy sight, and am no more worthy to be called thy son.* The father never let him finish the speech he rehearsed all the way home. He held that smelly, dirty, young man to his chest and cut him off verbally. He did not let him stay in that place where he felt like a failure. He more than restored him fully.

That is the same compassion we see on display in **Jer. 31:20 (KJV)** *"I will surely have mercy upon him saith the Lord."* His father never thought, "I might forgive but I won't forget, or he has to live with his bad choices." His heart cried out, "I want my child back, I want to fully restore." God was in the restoration business before the first rebellion split any relationship.

There is a song that expresses this so well Bethel Music recorded it by the title <u>Goodness of God</u>. The lyrics speak of the faithfulness of God, His love and goodness constantly reaching out to the brokenhearted. "His goodness came running after me." Our God did not just accept us but He sought us out and came running the moment we turned toward Him. God loved us first. He watched over us and longed for us to turn back towards Him. When we were ready for salvation, God met us more than half way. He made a bridge from the cross to welcome us home.

We can easily see the heart of our heavenly Father is expressed through this man, but most of us do not realize how very much God loves us. We do not come to a Father that will grudgingly forgive, but to our Abba, to our loving Father, who is eager to draw us near. **Luke 15:22 (KJV)** *²² But the father said to his servants, Bring forth the best robe, and put it on him; and put a ring on his hand, and shoes on his feet:* "Do you realize that God is never described as being in a hurry in the Bible? The only time He is portrayed as being in a hurry is in this story…He was in a hurry to clothe his son with the best robe—the robe of righteousness—placed on us. In doing so he reinstated us as sons of the Most High God, a position which we had lost when Adam fell. That father was in a hurry to put a ring on his son's hand. Like the authority that is invested in the signet ring of a rich man's son, our Father is eager to put back into our hands the authority to invoke His name, so that we can walk in dominion every day. The father was in a hurry to put sandals on his son's feet to assure him that he was still his son—only servants went about barefoot. Our Father never wants us to feel like hired servants or outcast. We are always His sons." (Prince 11/2/19)

Luke 15:23-24 (KJV) *²³ And bring hither the fatted calf, and kill it; and let us eat, and be merry: ²⁴ For this my son was dead, and is alive again; he was lost, and is found. And they began to be merry.* That is love. That man showed such compassion and understanding and forgiveness. He was looking for a way to restore all that was lost and heal all that was broken. It is what our heavenly Father does for each of His wayward children. God is seen as celebrating the lost ones that come home. Our Father rejoices over us, the implication is that He sings and dances over our return. What a beautiful picture that is.

God knew that rebellion lurked in the heart of all His children. When Adam turned away from God, our Father never turned His heart away. Adam was just like our prodigal, saying I want to do it my way. Like Adam we think that maybe God doesn't want what is best for us. We wonder what He is holding out on us. What does God know that I have not seen? Why can't I be like Him? Since we are just like Adam, we taste of sin. We try to elevate our status and fall from grace. We try it our own way and it leads to shame and despair. **Genesis 3:8-11 (KJV)** *⁸ And they heard the voice of the LORD God walking in the garden in the cool of the day: and Adam and his wife hid themselves from the presence of the LORD God amongst the trees of the garden. ⁹ And the LORD God called unto Adam, and said unto him, Where art thou?* Just like when my grandchildren hide behind a chair and most of them is in plain sight, I pretend I cannot find them. I cry our "Where are you?" God knew exactly where they were, but they needed to see where they were. They were outside of the boundary of obedience. They were lost and they needed to see that. *¹⁰ And he said, I heard thy voice in the garden, and I was afraid, because I was naked; and I hid myself. ¹¹ And he said, Who told thee that thou wast naked? Hast thou eaten of the tree, whereof I commanded thee that thou shouldest not eat?* It was customary for God to walk with them; they had always run to Him until they sinned. Now shame and willful disobedience had led them down their own path. They are hiding from God's loving invitation to fellowship. They felt unworthy and it drove them from God; they had turned away and all the time God was trying to get them to turn to Him again. We have been trying to hide from God ever since that day.

God never wanted us to carry failure and guilt, never wanted us to hang our heads in shame and hide from His face. He wanted us free so He sent Jesus, His perfect Son, to die so that we could live free. **Romans 8:1 (KJV)** *1 There is therefore now no condemnation to them which are in Christ Jesus, who walk not after the flesh, but after the Spirit.* God intended for mankind to walk in forgiveness. He made a way to fully restore all who are lost. That was not a bandage that God put on after a surprising fall. God had always known that man would turn away and still He showered mankind with love. He made provision to turn man back to the place where we could look Him in the face. **Ephesians 1:4 (NKJV)** *4 just as He chose us in Him before the foundation of the world, that we should be holy and without blame before Him in love...* Peter wrote the same thing in I Peter 1:20 and it is even recorded in the last book of the Bible. **Revelation 13:8 (KJV)** *8 And all that dwell upon the earth shall worship him, whose names are not written in the book of life of the Lamb slain from the foundation of the world.* Before Adam fell, the Father had already accepted the blood of Jesus as payment for every sin.

Jesus paid for us to be able to come home from our time of rebellion. He restored us; when we could only barely hope to be servants. He called us His sons and daughters. How very much God loved us. We were all a prodigal at one time, like that young and foolish son, we ran off and tried to live our own way.

There was another son in the story, who was just as lost, but he appeared to be good and obedient. He wasn't the good son that everyone thought he was. He stayed home, did the work, never openly rebelled, but he was messed up too. His heart was not right either. Like many of us, his rebellion was less conspicuous. He did not recognize or appreciate the love of his father any more than his younger brother.

Luke 15:25-32 (KJV) *25 Now his elder son was in the field: and as he came and drew nigh to the house, he heard musick and dancing. 26 And he called one of the servants, and asked what these things meant. 27 And he said unto him, Thy brother is come; and thy father hath killed the fatted calf, because he hath received him safe and sound.* Here is another chance for him to show love and compassion for both his brother and his father, but he does not sigh in relief or rejoice. The one who should have been seeking to reconcile his brother and father reacts with indignation; He gets mad. *28 And he was angry, and would not go in: therefore came his father out, and intreated him.* The father had run to first the younger and now the older of his sons. He is always initiating the conversation entreating them to come in. *29 And he answering said to his father, Lo, these many years do I serve thee, neither transgressed I at any time thy commandment: and yet thou never gavest me a kid, that I might make merry with my friends: 30 But as soon as this thy son was come, which hath devoured thy living with harlots, thou hast killed for him the fatted calf. 31 And he said unto him, Son, thou art ever with me, and all that I have is thine.* That father was saying, "Don't you see that we still have that relationship? I love you and I am here for you; doesn't it mean anything at all to you?" You do not even need to ask to claim what is already given unto you. Back when the prodigal had left, he had legally given ownership to this son of all the land and animals and family riches. *32 It was meet that we should make merry, and be glad: for this thy brother was dead, and is alive again; and was lost, and is found.* "Have you, like the older son, failed to understand your Father's heart? Your heavenly Father already gave you a rich inheritance in Christ when you became His son. He wants you to know that you have received the Spirit of sonship [see Romans 8:15]. So call out to him 'Abba Father!' And know how much He loves you. Because you are His heir, all that He has is yours to enjoy today." (Prince 10/19/19)

The parable we call the prodigal son is really one of three. The first parable in this chapter was about the lost sheep and how the shepherd loved him so much that he left the 99 that were safe in the fold and searched and ran to find him and save him and bring him back home. Our God is telling us that even if we are the only one in danger, He will search for us and save us from all harm. He wants us more than the shepherd wanted his sheep and more than the woman wanted her coins. He came looking for you. God is in the restoration business. He is seeking us out and pouring out blessings upon us. In both of those other two parables we see the same quote. **Luke 15: 10 (KJV)** *[10] Likewise, I say unto you, there is joy in the presence of the angels of God over one sinner that repenteth.* God is forever faithful. He is pouring out His compassion and grace and waiting for us to come home. God rejoices in our turning back to His loving arms.

Ezekiel 34:11-12 & 15-16a (KJV) *[11] For thus saith the Lord GOD; Behold, I, even I, will both search my sheep, and seek them out. [12] As a shepherd seeketh out his flock in the day that he is among his sheep that are scattered; so will I seek out my sheep, and will deliver them out of all places where they have been scattered in the cloudy and dark day. ...[15] I will feed my flock, and I will cause them to lie down, saith the Lord GOD. [16] I will seek that which was lost, and bring again that which was driven away, and will bind up that which was broken, and will strengthen that which was sick:*

Saul of Tarsus was another lost sheep. He openly ravaged the church, killed and jailed the ones who had made their way back to the Father through Jesus. He seems so destructive, and angry, but the truth is he thought he was protecting the faith of his fathers. He was zealous, but wrong. He was against all who believed in the truth he did not understand. While Saul was on his way to attack more Christians, God was running after him. The heavenly Father was calling out to him "Saul where are you?" **Acts 9:6 (KJV)** *[6] And he trembling and astonished said, Lord, what wilt thou have me to do? And the Lord said unto him, Arise, and go into the city, and it shall be told thee what thou must do.*

Saul could have refused, he could have said no, but he turned toward Damascus and even though he had to be led by hand he went into the city and prayed and waited until God sent someone to bring him healing and acceptance. Later he said I am the least of all the apostles, not even worthy to be called an apostle, because I was so opposed to the church. I murdered believers, I arrested women and children who had found Jesus and sent them into prison. But God was so rich in mercy that His goodness ran to me, followed me, hunted me down on the road to destruction and pulled me from death into life. That was the Apostle Paul's testimony. It is also my story and yours, maybe not exactly, but in essence, we were all going the wrong way and God came running after us, seeking us out and with open arms welcomed us home

Luke 19:10 (KJV) [10] *For the Son of man is come to seek and to save that which was lost.* Your Father has been watching for you, ready to do whatever it takes to bring you into the place of honor He intended for you. This time the older brother was willing even eager to help. Jesus came to restore fellowship, and intimacy. He went to great lengths to redeem His family. He gave His very life to save us, and He celebrates us, rejoices over us. Come home, not just out of sin, not just as a servant but return unto the Lord. Take one step forward towards that place where you and He were free to fellowship one with the other, and He will come running, grace and goodness in hand to receive and restore you. His faithfulness and love have never wavered.

Acts 4:13 (KJV) [13] *Now when they saw the boldness of Peter and John, and perceived that they were unlearned and ignorant men, they marvelled; and they took knowledge of them, that they had been with Jesus.*

What do you see?

When my daughter Amy bought a new house it needed a lot of updates. She came in and started to look with expectation at what it would be in the end. I remember her friend saying it has good bones. Amy did not look at the outdated carpet and wallpaper; she had an image of what it would be in her heart. She could see it finished. For her it was a new start, everything was changing, paint and lights and furnishings and when it was over it would be her house, as if no one had ever lived there before. A few months later, everyone could see with their eyes what she saw in her heart the whole time.

We have to do that in the spirit too. We have to look past what is and see what God sees. The devil tried to make Peter ashamed, reminding him of his denial. When he denied Jesus, it was because he could not see the real life that was eternity; he could only see the danger before him. There came a time when he looked at his past and then he looked at the cross and the empty tomb and moved on. It was true Peter had said he didn't even know Jesus, there really was danger of being arrested and killed, but later he stood up to lead the new believers. How we see ourselves matters, because we can be victims or victors. We can let our past and even our present become prison walls or stepping stones.

Acts 4:13 (KJV) *13 Now when they saw the boldness of Peter and John, and perceived that they were unlearned and ignorant men, they marvelled; and they took knowledge of them, that they had been with Jesus.* The men who opposed these two men arrested for preaching the gospel saw something in them. Relationship changed them. Peter and John could have looked at their past and said what are we doing, we are just fishermen, but they kept seeing Jesus and it made them better men, bolder men. There was so much power on Peter that hundreds brought sick people into the streets because if even his shadow fell on them they would be healed. Notoriety brought danger and opportunity.

Acts 5:17-20 (KJV) *₁₇ Then the high priest rose up, and all they that were with him, (which is the sect of the Sadducees,) and were filled with indignation, ₁₈ And laid their hands on the apostles, and put them in the common prison. ₁₉ But the angel of the Lord by night opened the prison doors, and brought them forth, and said, ₂₀ Go, stand and speak in the temple to the people all the words of this life.* That angel told them to go back and do the same thing that just got them arrested. The Lord supernaturally got him out of prison in this instance and again in Acts 12. No earthly enemy can stop what God has planned.

The devil tried to destroy the new believers with threats of prison. They refused to cower in fear. When the believers continued to thrive in the face of adversity, Satan sent a man named Saul of Tarsus. But after arresting and killing Christians Paul became one himself. Paul had such an anointing, and such a vision of the difference that Jesus could make in a life, that he covered most of the known world and everywhere he went he either started a church or a riot. No place was left as it was before he came. Salvation changed his outlook and his destiny. He was arrested and beaten repeatedly and yet he would not be silent. He was a voice shouting that Jesus had risen from the dead victorious over sin and that all men could be forgiven.

The Jewish leaders tried to discourage him and wanted to silence the message of Christ but all they did was give him a new platform on which to share the good news. Here we see Paul and Silas in trouble for setting a woman free from an evil spirit. **Acts 16:23-25 (KJV)** *₂₃ And when they had laid many stripes upon them, they cast them into prison, charging the jailor to keep them safely: ₂₄ Who, having received such a charge, thrust them into the inner prison, and made their feet fast in the stocks. ₂₅ And at midnight Paul and Silas prayed, and sang praises unto God: and the prisoners heard them.* There was no reason in the natural so sing. Times were bad, they were in pain, they were in prison and yet their hearts cried out to God. They could sing because they saw the Lord, not the prison bars. They didn't see suffering they saw an opportunity to worship and witness.

When a believer worships it changes the atmosphere. Things change in the spirit world and then sometimes things change in the natural world as well. **Acts 16:26-27 (KJV)** *26 And suddenly there was a great earthquake, so that the foundations of the prison were shaken: and immediately all the doors were opened, and every one's bands were loosed. 27 And the keeper of the prison awaking out of his sleep, and seeing the prison doors open, he drew out his sword, and would have killed himself, supposing that the prisoners had been fled.* I love it that not just Paul and Silas were released, but every man was loosed from his chains. Your worship can set prisoners free too.

If a prisoner escaped the jailor would have been executed. The Romans made it clear that it was his life for theirs if any escaped. Knowing the severity of their sentence against him and the terror of their methods of execution, suicide seemed preferable. **Acts 16:28-31 (KJV)** *28 But Paul cried with a loud voice, saying, Do thyself no harm: for we are all here. 29 Then he called for a light, and sprang in, and came trembling, and fell down before Paul and Silas, 30 And brought them out, and said, Sirs, what must I do to be saved? 31 And they said, Believe on the Lord Jesus Christ, and thou shalt be saved, and thy house.* The prisoners are telling the jailor how to be free; I find some irony there. There was revival in that prison. And then they went out of the prison and into the home of their jailor and ministered the word of salvation to all his family and servants.

Acts 16:32-34 (KJV) *32 And they spake unto him the word of the Lord, and to all that were in his house. 33 And he took them the same hour of the night, and washed their stripes; and was baptized, he and all his, straightway. 34 And when he had brought them into his house, he set meat before them, and rejoiced, believing in God with all his house.* Since Paul has now finished the task God had for him in that jail, the word comes that he can be released. Paul made them come and release him personally with great apology before he would leave that prison. Because he saw relationship with Jesus as vitally important, he was never ashamed. No prison ever got him distracted from his goal. Paul looked beyond the walls and saw the kingdom of God. He kept his eye on the target.

Paul assumed the commission to preach on the streets and in the prisons and in the courtroom. He recognized the danger and then looked at the souls around him in more danger and saw an opportunity for men to be saved no matter what the cost. **II Timothy 2:9-11 (KJV)** *9 Wherein I suffer trouble, as an evil doer, even unto bonds; but the word of God is not bound. 10 Therefore I endure all things for the elect's sakes, that they may also obtain the salvation which is in Christ Jesus with eternal glory. 11 It is a faithful saying: For if we be dead with him, we shall also live with him:*

When the world looked at the Apostles, they did not say these are just fishermen or even a persecutor of the church turned evangelist. They saw men of faith as dangerous. **Acts 17:6b (KJV)** *6b These that have turned the world upside down are come hither also*; Could they honestly say that about us? These are the ones who minister to the poor and touch the broken hearted and feed the hungry and they honestly help and encourage wherever they go. The day has come when it is not all that politically correct to mention the name of Jesus, but hopefully there is abundant proof that we belong to Him. We can see how dark the world is becoming or like Paul we can be the light.

David wrote about the struggle between men and the deliverance of who stand with God. **Psalm 56:1-11 (KJV)** *1 Be merciful unto me, O God: for man would swallow me up; he fighting daily oppresseth me. 2 Mine enemies would daily swallow me up: for they be many that fight against me, O thou most High. 3 What time I am afraid, I will trust in thee. 4 In God I will praise his word, in God I have put my trust; I will not fear what flesh can do unto me. 5 Every day they wrest my words: all their thoughts are against me for evil. 6 They gather themselves together, they hide themselves, they mark my steps, when they wait for my soul. 7 Shall they escape by iniquity? in thine anger cast down the people, O God. 8 Thou tellest my wanderings: put thou my tears into thy* *bottle: are they not in thy book?* ⁹ *When I cry unto thee, then shall mine enemies turn back: this I know; for God is for me.* ¹⁰ *In God will I praise his word: in the LORD will I praise his word.* ¹¹ *In God have I put my trust: I will not be afraid what man can do unto me.* I can relate a little to what David said, and while I might not have been thrown into prison, I am a little like Peter and Paul in that I will not go quietly. I might be singing in the dark, but I won't just lie down and take it.

When Jesus entered Jerusalem the crowds praised Him and immediately the religious leaders complained. **Luke 19:40 (KJV)** ⁴⁰ *And he answered and said unto them, I tell you that, if these should hold their peace, the stones would immediately cry out.* If we keep silent and refuse to speak up because of what we see around us God will raise up another voice. No rock is going to take my place, I will praise Him. I will bear witness of His greatness. I will see with the eye of faith, looking beyond the here and now into what will be. I will have a vision clear enough to help someone else see Him.

What do you see? You can see trouble and fear and danger all around you. You can see lack and failure and weakness, or you can see Jesus standing with you, helping you, delivering you and bringing you into a future that words fail to describe. You can see your own ability and knowledge or you can see the miraculous. Jesus is still alive, He is still powerful and He wants you to walk out all that He has spoken unto you until the day of His return. Take hold of what Jesus spoke over you. Place that as your target and aim at it. Pull back on that bow and let the arrows fly. Your faith and confidence will flourish as you firmly plant your trust in Him and focus on what He has placed in your heart. Nothing could stop Peter or Paul and nothing can stop you. Let the eye of faith keep you on target for victory.

Romans 3:24-25 (KJV) *²⁴ Being justified freely by his grace through the redemption that is in Christ Jesus: ²⁵ Whom God hath set forth to be a propitiation through faith in his blood, to declare his righteousness for the remission of sins that are past, through the forbearance of God;*

Stop Trying So Hard

As Christians we can either work to try to be good enough and to never make a mistake, or we can trust in what Jesus has done and recognize that we do not have to earn anything with God. We do not have standing based upon our efforts, but rather based upon the blood of Jesus who came to redeem us.

While the idea of redemption was introduced in the Old Testament it became complete in what Jesus did for us. Redemption is a sacrifice centered term that the Hebrews understood as related to their law. The idea of real salvation, truly taking mankind out of bondage and into a state of acceptance was still foreign to many Jews, and so referring to Jesus as the One who redeems was an important concept. They had to know that their debt was paid in full and that through the blood of Jesus they could now walk with God without a sense of shame and regret. They had to take by faith something they had tried to obtain through hundreds of years of effort. To be a purchased possession of God was a precious thought. To be once and for all forgiven was new to them.

God does not focus on how much I read or pray or work for the church. He is not concerned with the amount of my tithes and offerings. He does not focus on any achievement or effort, but rather on my continual trust in the finished work of Christ. God is not urging me to try harder; what He really wants is for me to just love Him and let Him love me. God's emphasis is on relationship not effort.

Jesus bought and paid for us in a way that made mankind free by virtue of a one-time offering of God's perfect sacrifice— that is, His own Son. **Colossians 2:13-15 (KJV)** [13] *And you, being* *dead in your sins and the uncircumcision of your flesh, hath he quickened together with him, having forgiven you all trespasses;* [14] *Blotting out the handwriting of ordinances that was against us, which was contrary to us, and took it out of the way, nailing it to his cross;* [15] *And having spoiled principalities and powers, he made a shew of them openly, triumphing over them in it.* In the time this was written, men understood the sin-debt in a way that we overlook. During their time, if a man owed a huge debt, more than he could possibly pay, he could hope for mercy and help by openly displaying his shameful insufficiencies. That man would humble himself by placing his debt on public display. Usually a copy of his unpaid debt was nailed to his doorpost. The hope was that someone of great wealth and compassion would take pity on him and pay the debt before he was sold into slavery or sent to prison. If that happened, it was evident by the fact that a benefactor would take the note and fold it over, hiding the amount owed. That symbolized that this man was now free, no further payment was required and no shame was attached to his failure to pay. He hasn't filed bankruptcy; his debt was paid in full. When Jesus hung on the cross, He took His own blood and blotted out the list of accusations, and the full sin-debt that we owed. Jesus took all of our spiritual failure and nailed it to His cross. The whole list of our debt, the wages of sin—which was death was finally paid when He died in my place. When Jesus said, "It is finished." All I owed was gone. He paid in full for my freedom and restored my honor with His own righteousness.

The whole of Galatians chapter 3 tells us that God no longer puts men in the bondage of struggling against their own sinful nature. Paul makes it clear that the just, those who are accepted as if they had not sinned, were living daily by faith. **Galatians 3:13-14 (KJV)** [13] *Christ hath redeemed. us from the curse of the law, being made a curse for us: for it is written, Cursed is every one that hangeth on a tree*: That word redeemed means to buy back, to rescue from loss, and to improve opportunity. [14] *That the blessing of Abraham might come on the Gentiles through Jesus Christ; that we might receive the promise of the Spirit through faith.* The law was a teaching tool to show us where we had failed and how much we needed someone to do what we could not do. Because Jesus was the only man who had ever satisfied the demands of the Law, He could finally bring those who never obeyed it to God just as if they had never sinned. Jesus redeemed us with the highest of prices, His own blood. He paid in full the debt and penalty of sin and death. He bore within His own body my sin, carried all my failures and wrong actions and thoughts in His heart and made me free. I just see Him as the perfect substitute sacrifice and take what He did as if it was for me alone and I am free from judgement, from fear of failure, from condemnation and guilt. I died in a sense with Jesus on that cross and I never have to fear spiritual death and the punishment that I would have rightfully deserved.

The innocent Jesus took my place, paid my debt, purchased my freedom, and I am so glad He did. Paul was showing these men who had tried their whole lives to follow the law and falling short there was a new way. They had lived under constant condemnation. Paul showed them that there was no longer a way to reach God through their efforts, the whole of legalism was a waste of time. No man could ever constantly and continually do what was right or good. Man's nature was tainted by the sin of Adam and every one of us fell into sin's trap. The more laws and restrictions that were set up the more times they knew they didn't measure up. The law included every aspect of man, not just actions, but even the intents and attitudes of man. Paul was such a zealous Jew that he was driven to destroy those who found faith; his motive was pure but his actions were evil. He said, "I was the worst of sinners because I persecuted the church, but I never knew I could rest on the blood of Jesus and His obedience rather than seek out my own righteousness."

I can hear relief in the voice of Paul as he penned this letter to Timothy. **I Timothy 1:12-15 (KJV)** *12 And I thank Christ Jesus our Lord, who hath enabled me, for that he counted me faithful, putting me into the ministry; 13 Who was before a blasphemer, and a persecutor, and injurious: but I obtained mercy, because I did it ignorantly in unbelief. 14 And the grace of our Lord was exceeding* *abundant with faith and love which is in Christ Jesus.* ¹⁵ *This is a faithful saying, and worthy of all acceptation, that Christ Jesus came into the world to save sinners; of whom I am chief.* There is no man, woman or child that has ever sinned so severely that the blood is not enough to make them clean. There is no further effort needed to earn God's love and mercy; it is already ours. We do not obey to get approval but we live a good life out of our relationship. God loved us, and Christ redeemed us, so now we who are showered in forgiveness, in grace, and mercy live well because we can, not because we have to. There is great freedom in not having every thought and actions take us out of favor. For the Jews, the struggle against their nature, the whole of legalism, led to one continuous state of condemnation and a sense of failure. Now that we are no longer slaves to sin, we can live free. I am not saying that we do not honor God with the life He redeemed; rather we love Him because He loved us. We can now know Him enough to want to please Him and still know that even when we don't, His love for us is not effected by our behavior.

Romans 3:20-25 (KJV) ²⁰ *Therefore by the deeds of the law there shall no flesh be justified in his sight: for by the law is the knowledge of sin.* ²¹ *But now the righteousness of God without the law is manifested, being witnessed by the law and the prophets;* ²² *Even the righteousness of God which is by faith* ²³ *For all have sinned, and come short of the glory of God;* ²⁴ *Being justified freely by his grace through the redemption that is in Christ Jesus:* ²⁵ *Whom God hath set forth to be a propitiation through faith in his blood, to declare his righteousness for the remission of sins that are past, through the forbearance of God;*

What freedom there is in knowing that while I sinned, His love was too strong to leave me under the penalty of my actions. His blood washed me so clean that it is as if I had never sinned. That is what justification is. I am free because of an imparted sense of righteousness. God must truly love us to take the holiness of Christ and apply it to our weak and flawed lives.

God laid all of the weight of our past and even our current failures and sins upon Jesus. **Romans 5:1 (KJV)** *1 Therefore being justified by faith, we have peace with God through our Lord Jesus Christ:* Not only do we have peace, but we also have joy and confidence, because we have nothing to prove and nothing to earn. God made us free. Jesus made us pure and holy.

I Peter 1:18-21 (KJV) *18 Forasmuch as ye know that ye were not redeemed with corruptible things, as silver and gold, from your vain conversation received by tradition from your fathers; 19 But with the precious blood of Christ, as of a lamb without blemish and without spot: 20 Who verily was foreordained before the foundation of the world, but was manifest in these last times for you, 21 Who by him do believe in God, that raised him up from the dead, and gave him glory; that your faith and hope might be in God.* God took the most precious thing in all of creation, His own Son's blood and purchased our redemption. Nothing has more value than that blood and He freely gave it for us. His love compelled Him to offer whatever was needed to bring us safely into a place where we could fellowship with Him. Our Father valued us highly. He believed we were worth the price He paid.

Every believer has part in the shed blood and is now free to stand in the presence of a holy God. From both heaven and earth there is honor for the One who has redeemed us. **Revelation 5:9-10 (KJV)** *9 And they sung a new song, saying, Thou art worthy to take the book, and to open the seals thereof: for thou wast slain, and hast redeemed us to God by thy blood out of every kindred, and tongue, and people, and nation; 10 And hast made us unto our God kings and priests: and we shall reign on the earth.* That word for redeem, means to buy back, to go to the market—that is to intentionally go for the purpose of purchasing. The whole reason Christ came was to redeem us.

When I was first saved it was pounded into my head, that "I am just a sinner, saved by grace." That is not really accurate. I was a sinner in need of a Savior, but now I am saved. Jesus paid to change my very nature. I no longer identify as a sinner; I see myself through the gift of salvation as whole and pure and clean. My daily actions do not add to or subtract from the perfect gift of grace poured out to me. I am bought with a price, chosen of God and perfect in His eyes by virtue of the blood alone.

If then we know that He redeemed us, and He purposed to make us free, we are free. We should know it in such detail that we no longer think of ourselves as sinners and failures but we think of ourselves as free, forgiven, and purchased by the precious blood of God's only Son.

Romans 8:1-10 (KJV) *1 There is therefore now no condemnation to them which are in Christ Jesus, who walk not after the flesh, but after the Spirit.* If we really believe that the Redeemer came and saved us we should not live under a shadow of shame. There is no longer a death sentence hanging over us. There is no longer a sense of guilt and condemnation on us. *2 For the law of the Spirit of life in Christ Jesus hath made me free from the law of sin and death. 3 For what the law could not do, in that it was weak through the flesh, God sending his own Son in the likeness of sinful flesh, and for sin, condemned sin in the flesh:* The struggle to be right, to do right, to follow every law and rule and ordinance was impossible for fallen mankind. Therefore, God said "I will pay for the sin and failure myself; I will provide a sacrifice that is acceptable and send the only One who can fulfill the law." You do not have to be perfect in and of yourself because Jesus is perfect and He has taken your place. *4 That the righteousness of the law might be fulfilled in us, who walk not after the flesh, but after the Spirit.* That does not mean you are always in prayer and continually walking in the anointing. It does not mean you never give in to your body. It does not mean that you always do good; it means that you remain in the place of redemption. That same spirit that raised Jesus from the dead is in you and you walk out your days aware of Him. You are not trying and trying to be what you can never attain on your own but you are saved and you know it. *5 For they that are after the flesh do mind the things of the flesh; but they that are after the Spirit the things of the Spirit. 6 For to be carnally minded is death; but to be spiritually minded is life* *and peace. ⁷Because the carnal mind is enmity against God: for it is not subject to the law of God, neither indeed can be. ⁸So then they that are in the flesh cannot please God. ⁹But ye are not in the flesh, but in the Spirit, if so be that the Spirit of God dwell in you.* He said a couple of good things there. First Paul tells us that before we were saved all we could do was surrender to our flesh and temptations led us into sin because sin ruled us. But now that we are saved, our thinking changes and we care that we live right. We do not do it by doubling up our efforts, but by leaning hard on our relationship. We nurture our spirit man so that spirit inside us can help us to live daily dependent upon His grace, without stress and strain. I know that we don't follow perfectly but we are still following Him. His Holy Spirit lives in us to help us daily. *..Now if any man have not the Spirit of Christ, he is none of his. ¹⁰And if Christ be in you, the body is dead because of sin; but the Spirit is life because of righteousness.*

God has made us righteous. We cannot try to become what we already are. Once seated in a chair we do not continue to try to sit down, we rest in it. In the same way, we know that we are what He has made us. He has changed our nature and character and looks upon us through the sacrifice of Christ and sees us as what Jesus has made us. In fact, He sees us exactly like He sees Jesus. That is a lot of grace and mercy on His part. He makes us both whole and holy. We could not earn it and could not do it on our own. It is applied to us, imparted to us. He is the Lord our Righteousness! **Jeremiah 23:4-6 (KJV)** *⁴And I will set up shepherds over them which shall feed them: and they shall fear no more, nor be dismayed, neither shall they be lacking, saith the LORD. ⁵Behold, the days come, saith the LORD, that I will raise unto David a righteous Branch, and a King shall reign and prosper, and shall execute judgment and justice in the earth. ⁶In his days Judah shall be saved, and Israel shall dwell safely: and this is his name whereby he shall be called, THE LORD OUR RIGHTEOUSNESS.* He is the Lord Jehovah who makes us righteous—the Messiah, and His name is Jesus.

He alone was righteous and just and so He alone could make us that. For us to have any ability to do anything good, or for us to obey at all, required His nature and character. That is exactly what happened at the new birth. Our old man died and we were born again, changed into one like Our Father. God now lives within us and that makes us able to stand in the presence of a holy God unashamed and untainted by sin. We should be fully aware of His righteousness within us and that overshadows all of our efforts and failures.

Hebrews 10:1-10 (KJV) *1 For the law having a shadow of good things to come, and not the very image of the things, can never with those sacrifices which they offered year by year continually make the comers thereunto perfect. 2 For then would they not have ceased to be offered? because that the worshippers once purged should have had no more conscience of sins.* That is where we should be now, fully aware of His sacrifice, no longer dependent upon our own works, but recognizing that we have no reason to carry around a guilty conscience. *3 But in those sacrifices there is a remembrance again made of sins every year. 4 For it is not possible that the blood of bulls and of goats should take away sins. 5 Wherefore when he cometh into the world, he saith, Sacrifice and offering thou wouldest not, but a body hast thou prepared me: 6 In burnt offerings and sacrifices for sin thou hast had no pleasure. 7 Then said I, Lo, I come (in the volume of the book it is written of me,) to do thy will, O God. 8 Above when he said, Sacrifice and offering and burnt offerings and offering for sin thou wouldest not, neither hadst pleasure therein; which are offered by the law; 9 Then said he, Lo, I come to do thy will, O God. He taketh away the first, that he may establish the second. 10 By the which will we are sanctified through the offering of the body of Jesus Christ once for all.* We are made holy; it is not we who accomplish anything, because He has already done it.

Romans 4:13-25 (KJV) *13 For the promise, that he should be the heir of the world, was not to Abraham, or to his seed,* The promise was not to the natural born son, Isaac, but to the whole of the generations that would receive the benefit of the one true seed

Jesus—that means you are part of those who became the seed. *13 For the promise, that he should be the heir of the world, was not to Abraham, or to his seed, through the law, but through the righteousness of faith. 14 For if they which are of the law be heirs, faith is made void, and the promise made of none effect... 16 Therefore it is of faith, that it might be by grace; to the end the promise might be sure to all the seed...* To everyone who is now part of the body of Christ, *21 And being fully persuaded that, what he had promised, he was able also to perform. 22 And therefore it was imputed to him for righteousness. 23 Now it was not written for his sake alone, that it was imputed to him; 24 But for us also, to whom it shall be imputed, if we believe on him that raised up Jesus our Lord from the dead; 25 Who was delivered for our offences, and was raised again for our justification.* That word justification means we have been granted acquittal for Christ's sake, as if we had never sinned.

Ephesians 5:25-27 (KJV) *25 Husbands, love your wives, even as Christ also loved the church, and gave himself for it; 26 That he might sanctify and cleanse it with the washing of water by the word, 27 That he might present it to himself a glorious church, not having spot, or wrinkle, or any such thing; but that it should be holy and without blemish.* The Lord sees us holy, and sees us perfect even when we are less than our best. We do not have to rely upon our own good deeds but we rest assured of our salvation and know that He sees in us what we have never seen in ourselves. In the eyes of God, we are perfect, holy, and washed clean. We have no stain of sin, no flaw, we are a glorious church with no spot, no wrinkle, no sin, or failure, if we confidently trust in the blood that makes us clean. It is the only way we can begin to live well. Now that we know we are free we can refuse to walk in the ways of sinfulness because we are finally able to stand in God's presence.

This is how we resist the devil and sin, we see ourselves in Christ; we are both dead unto sin and alive unto God. We remember who He is and what He did and we see ourselves pure and holy and clean because of Him. **Romans 6:1-18 (KJV)** *1 What* *shall we say then? Shall we continue in sin, that grace may abound?* ²*God forbid. How shall we, that are dead to sin, live any longer therein?* ³*Know ye not, that so many of us as were baptized into Jesus Christ were baptized into his death? ...* ⁶*Knowing this, that our old man is crucified with him, that the body of sin might be destroyed, that henceforth we should not serve sin.* ⁷*For he that is dead is freed from sin.* ⁸*Now if we be dead with Christ, we believe that we shall also live with him:* ¹¹*Likewise reckon ye also yourselves to be dead indeed unto sin, but alive unto God through Jesus Christ our Lord.* ¹²*Let not sin therefore reign in your mortal body, that ye should obey it in the lusts thereof.* ¹³*Neither yield ye your members as instruments of unrighteousness unto sin: but yield yourselves unto God, as those that are alive from the dead, and your members as instruments of righteousness unto God.* ¹⁴*For sin shall not have dominion over you: for ye are not under the law, but under grace...* ¹⁸*Being then made free from sin, ye became the servants of righteousness.*

We are no longer bound to sin because of Jesus; that makes us free. We are the righteousness of God in Christ Jesus. We can rest in that fact; we can anchor our souls in that. We know who we are because of whose we are and that makes us righteous.

So stop trying so hard and learn to rest in Him alone. **Hebrews 4:9-10 (KJV)** ⁹*There remaineth therefore a rest to the people of God.* ¹⁰*For he that is entered into his rest, he also hath ceased from his own works, as God did from his.* What a relief it is to know I do not have to be perfect, because I am definitely not perfect. I just lean on His righteousness and do what He says knowing that His grace, His mercy, His blood is enough!

Proverbs 19:17 (KJV) *¹⁷ He that hath pity upon the poor lendeth unto the LORD; and that which he hath given will he pay him again.*

Lending to the Lord

Compassion was one of the strongest characteristics we see in the ministry of Christ. By just looking at the four gospels we can know that ministry to the sick and needy is very much at the heart of God. It was compassion that raised the widow's son and the daughter of Jairus. It was compassion that reached out and touched the leper before Jesus healed him. It was a deep desire to minister to the lost that drove first Jesus and then His disciples to travel for miles just to free one demonic or a damaged, rejected woman at the well. The heart of our Lord cared deeply about the sinner, the weary, the broken, and the sinful soul. So wherever He went, those people had His attention and His help.

Jesus cared so much for the poor and needy that He made it a priority for those that please Him. When He spoke of those blessed at the end of the age, He used this passage. **Matthew 25:35-40 (KJV)** *35 For I was an hungred, and ye gave me meat: I was thirsty, and ye gave me drink: I was a stranger, and ye took me in: 36 Naked, and ye clothed me: I was sick, and ye visited me: I was in prison, and ye came unto me. 37 Then shall the righteous answer him, saying, Lord, when saw we thee an hungred, and fed thee? or thirsty, and gave thee drink? 38 When saw we thee a stranger, and took thee in? or naked, and clothed thee? 39 Or when saw we thee sick, or in prison, and came unto thee? 40 And the King shall answer and say unto them, Verily I say unto you, Inasmuch as ye have done it unto one of the least of these my brethren, ye have done it unto me.*

Scripture confirms His interest in meeting the needs of the poor. **Proverbs 19:17 (KJV)** *17 He that hath pity upon the poor lendeth unto the LORD; and that which he hath given will he pay him again.* God established a generous circle in which He supplies so we can minister and then He restocks the supply so we can do it again and again.

He has proven that for years to the members of the House of Victory. When we started the food pantry it was just a desire in the heart of one woman who knew there were hungry, needy people around us. Our church is in an impoverished area. In the beginning we only had a few shelves of food and people would hear about us through word of mouth and come and pick up a bag or two of groceries. Then the vision grew and people started to bring in food for the poor. Now we post our food pantry hours on Facebook and tell everyone we can that there is food for the asking. We believed we would be feeding the homeless and we have at times. But mostly, we feed the underemployed who are struggling or the grandparents who are suddenly raising a second generation of children on Social Security. Jesus said there would always be poor among us and He was right. There are people with needs are all around us. As believers it is our obligation and our honor to minister where we can.

When someone comes into the food pantry, we try to make them feel important, loved and wanted. We greet them like long lost friends and offer them coffee and donuts while they fill out their grocery list. They get to choose what they want from the things we have. We receive no government subsidies so we do not require ID or proof of need. We know there are people who could not qualify for food stamps but went to bed hungry and we understand that other places have a reason for what they do, but we trust God to supply and we do our best to minister to anyone who walks in the doors. We also have sources that just show up so that there is extra bread and sometimes fresh fruits and vegetables. The church buys some food but our members also bring it in. We have found favor with other ministries that send us cases of food, without our asking, whenever things get scarce. It is beautiful to see how God supplies. Our church of less than 70 people feeds about 25 hungry families every week. Since the Lord was full of compassion it is only right that His children are as well.

Mark 6:34-44 (KJV) *34 And Jesus, when he came out, saw much people, and was moved with compassion toward them, because they were as sheep not having a shepherd: and he began to teach them many things. 35 And when the day was now far spent, his disciples came unto him, and said, This is a desert place, and now the time is far passed: 36 Send them away, that they may go into the country round about, and into the villages, and buy themselves bread: for they have nothing to eat. 37 He answered and said unto them, Give ye them to eat. And they say unto him, Shall we go and buy two hundred pennyworth of bread, and give them to eat? 38 He saith unto them, How many loaves have ye? go and see. And when they knew, they say, Five, and two fishes.* Think about this; that was not enough food for the disciples to eat. It was just a small boy's lunch. I have heard it compared to a couple of sardines and a handful of biscuits. Jesus did not seem concerned about how His followers were going to eat, but He had compassion on the crowd of seekers. *39 And he commanded them to make all sit down by companies upon the green grass. 40 And they sat down in ranks, by hundreds, and by fifties. 41 And when he had taken the five loaves and the two fishes, he looked up to heaven, and blessed, and brake the loaves, and gave them to his disciples to set before them; and the two fishes divided he among them all. 42 And they did all eat, and were filled. 43 And they took up twelve baskets full of the fragments, and of the fishes. 44 And they that did eat of the loaves were about five thousand men.* It was more than enough for 5000 men not to mentions wives and children and the disciples themselves.

God who cares for the forsaken and needy has a way of putting food into our hands so we always have enough to share. Our food pantry isn't exactly the miracle of fish and loaves for the 5000, but it feels like that sometimes. If we get a huge donation from the library or post office food drive it means we are going to see more needy people than usual. If we have extra food in the pantry it might find its way into our after school free snacks or a military box to bless our troops. Sometimes it goes to a drug rehab in another city, or a street ministry. Just yesterday we received several boxes of baby food. We were able to funnel most of it into a parenting group for needy mothers. The truth is we are just a conduit. We have been both the source for other ministries and the recipients from them. God is so good to touch the lives of the needy around us, and sometimes He lets us help.

There is always enough in God's storehouse for any who are willing to ask and minister with His help. **I John 3:17-19 (KJV)** *17 But whoso hath this world's good, and seeth his brother have need, and shutteth up his bowels of compassion from him, how dwelleth the love of God in him? 18 My little children, let us not love in word, neither in tongue; but in deed and in truth. 19 And hereby we know that we are of the truth, and shall assure our hearts before him.*

Maybe your church doesn't have any outreach to the needy. There must be something you can do. What about a few random acts of kindness? I personally have left groceries on a porch of someone in need, and driven away; no one ever knew it was me. It feels really good to do that. Or you could just pay for an extra coffee or soda or gas when you are getting your own. Buy for the car behind you at the drive through. Once when I felt led to do that, the order behind me was more than I expected and I came up $.07 short and the cashier was so excited to put in that change. We both nearly cried at the joy of blessing a stranger. When I drove away I was thankful that I could not just do it alone, because that girl working for minimum wage got to help. There are a million ways to reach out and touch someone. I carry a Ziploc bag of snacks in my car with a few dollars inside in case I see hungry people on the streets asking for help. We need to learn to be sensitive to Holy Spirit prompting us. "One reason believers fail to follow their heart is that they have become too busy with natural affairs to get quiet inside and listen to what the Holy Spirit is saying to their spirit." (Hagin p. 62) If we ask Him, God will show us ways to be a blessing.

It doesn't have to be formal ministry to matter. If you don't have money you could shovel a driveway for the elderly person next door or mow their grass. Offer to watch a baby while a weary mom just takes a breath. What about going to the closest school and offering to volunteer? My mom used to volunteer at the hospital, she had no real skills but she would quietly sit and hold crying babies. If you sew, do some mending for someone who doesn't have the skills or a sewing machine. We all have some time or talent to share. There are street crews working in the heat who would be overjoyed if you walked up to them with cold tea or lemonade. That new girl at church, who wears the same thing every week, might love something extra from your closet. If you have a phone it takes a minute to call or text someone to remind them that they are not alone. My point is this, there are needs all around us if we open our eyes and become sensitive to the promptings of God. Our church motto is help and encourage. It doesn't cost anything to be kind, to listen, to smile or hold a door open. In this self-absorbed world those gestures matter. There were fourteen instances in the gospels where Jesus was said to have had compassion on someone and met their need. That seems to speak clearly that those acts of kindness mean something to our Father.

If God cared enough about a widow from Zarephath that He sent a prophet to miraculously provide for her for over a year, surely He cares about you and those around you. **Matthew 10:7-8 (KJV)** *7 And as ye go, preach, saying, The kingdom of heaven is at hand. 8 Heal the sick, cleanse the lepers, raise the dead, cast out devils: freely ye have received, freely give.* Maybe you can't heal the sick and raise the dead, but you can care. You can put in time and you can pray. That is truly the heart of God. He has never forsaken the lonely, the hungry the broken ones.

Matthew 10:42 (KJV) *42 And whosoever shall give to drink unto one of these little ones a cup of cold water only in the name of a disciple, verily I say unto you, he shall in no wise lose his reward.* God loves them through us sometimes; He always sees an act of kindness. What touches an earthly heart touches His heart and He touches ours. How precious that we can participate in those moments.

I want to always remember that the Lord has been gracious unto me. I could be the one on the street, homeless and hungry, but I am warm and fed and that is a wonderful thing. When we give to the needy, lend a hand, or offer to help it is His hand extended and He will use it for good. We cannot change the whole world, but we can touch those we have contact with. Aiming for the heart of God includes caring for the ones Jesus died for. I want to be part of that handful of believers who fed and clothed Him unknowingly. I want a heart full of compassion with eyes that see and the follow-through that meets the needs of others.

Aiming for the Heart of God

I Kings 18:44 (KJV) *⁴⁴And it came to pass at the seventh time, that he said, Behold, there ariseth a little cloud out of the sea, like a man's hand. And he said, Go up, say unto Ahab, Prepare thy chariot, and get thee down, that the rain stop thee not.*

After the Drought

Have you ever been really thirsty and dry spiritually? There are times when we all feel like we have been walking in the desert. When we think we are so parched and broken that we can never get satisfied again. Sometimes it is like we almost can't breathe, can't really pray. We are just going through the motions on auto pilot without feelings of intimacy with God. Our prayers are a list of requests as if God is unconcerned. That is never true. God is forever looking to bring us into His loving embrace. That does not mean we never feel alone because we all do sometimes.

John 7:37 (KJV) *37 In the last day, that great day of the feast, Jesus stood and cried, saying, If any man thirst, let him come unto me, and drink.* To drink spiritually means to take in and accept something until it becomes part of you. Just like water that enters in and becomes part of the very cells of the one who drinks. (Keller p. 41) Philip Keller wrote A Shepherd looks at Psalm 23 and he referred to the desperate need for the shepherd to make sure his sheep are well watered. Jesus is the Good Shepherd who watches to make sure we too are fed and well-watered. He surrounds us with ways to receive from His word.

Matthew 5:6 (KJV) *6 Blessed are they which do hunger and thirst after righteousness: for they shall be filled.* But sometimes we still feel thirsty and dry, and it can cause us to wander away. I read in the Bible that if all of His other sheep are safe in the fold; He will still come searching for me. **Matthew 18:12-14 (KJV)** *12 How think ye? if a man have an hundred sheep, and one of them be gone astray, doth he not leave the ninety and nine, and goeth into the mountains, and seeketh that which is gone astray? 13 And if so be that he find it, verily I say unto you, he rejoiceth more of that sheep, than of the ninety and nine which* *went not astray. ¹⁴ Even so it is not the will of your Father which is in heaven, that one of these little ones should perish.* He has such compassion on us that He would never abandon us in our sorrow or distress. We might feel like we are in the desert but the Great Shepherd of our souls is coming to guide us back to still waters.

We all know that Israel went through some deep struggles and there were times they felt as if God no longer carried them in His heart. They actually went through a physical drought that lasted over three years. They lived in a real desert climate, so no rain meant there were no crops. Their sheep were panting in fields without green grass. Their people were starving. The nation as a whole was being judged and Elijah told their leader Ahab there will be neither dew nor rain until I say so. Since those words came from God, He backed them up. The ground cracked, the streams dried up. Everything started to die. But God was still there. **I Kings 18:1(KJV)** ¹ *And it came to pass after many days, that the word of the LORD came to Elijah in the third year, saying, Go, shew thyself unto Ahab; and I will send rain upon the earth.* The nation had been judged because of idolatry, and then Elijah came and forced them into seeing the truth. He met with all the prophets of Baal on Mount Carmel and called down fire from heaven. Elijah proved that the Lord was still God in Israel and once he did the people acknowledged the truth. **I Kings 18:37-39 (KJV)** *³⁷ Hear me, O LORD, hear me, that this people may know that thou art the LORD God, and that thou hast turned their heart back again. ³⁸ Then the fire of the LORD fell, and consumed the burnt sacrifice, and the wood, and the stones, and the dust, and licked up the water that was in the trench. ³⁹ And when all the people saw it, they fell on their faces: and they said, The LORD, he is the God; the LORD, he is the God.* They shouted out in repentance and the curse was lifted.

Elijah killed all the false prophets and then he went to the king with good news. **I Kings 18:41 (KJV)** *⁴¹ And Elijah said unto Ahab, Get thee up, eat and drink; for there is a sound of abundance of rain.* No one else heard thunder. There were no clouds in the sky, but Elijah could sense it in the spirit. Something had changed in the atmosphere and now he could ask God to pardon the nation and lift the death sentence against them. He could pray for rain. He didn't say there would be a small shower. He said he heard the sound of torrents of rain. Elijah promised a gully-washer.

I Kings 18:42-43 (KJV) *42 So Ahab went up to eat and to drink. And Elijah went up to the top of Carmel; and he cast himself down upon the earth, and put his face between his knees,* Elijah knelt until he was face down in the dirt and he interceded for the people. When he prayed, he believed. Once he had prayed, he could act as if the rain was eminent. *43 And said to his servant, Go up now, look toward the sea. And he went up, and looked, and said, There is nothing. And he said, Go again seven times.* Elijah was not moved by how he felt. He did not let a negative report interfere with his faith. He said keep going back seven times and then come and tell me that the manifestation has come. *44 And it came to pass at the seventh time, that he said, Behold, there ariseth a little cloud out of the sea, like a man's hand.* The servant saw a tiny wisp of a cloud forming. He said it is so small I can hide it with my hand. The Lord was sending rain. It did not matter to Elijah that Ahab did not really believe or what his servant thought, what mattered is that God was visiting His people with rain. That tiny almost imperceptible cloud was God's proof that times refreshing were coming. **I Kings 18:44-45 (KJV)** *And he said, Go up, say unto Ahab, Prepare thy chariot, and get thee down, that the rain stop thee not. 45 And it came to pass in the meanwhile, that the heaven was black with clouds and wind, and there was a great rain. And Ahab rode, and went to Jezreel.* God spoke through His prophet, and even that faithless King started running to get off the mountain before the wind and clouds and raindrops started. Ahab caught the vision and drove down the mountain because he could imagine his chariot wheels stuck in the mud if he waited. Elijah saw it in the spirit while it was just a tiny cloud, but eventually everyone and everything got wet.

Maybe you have been walking in those dry valleys. God's faithfulness will carry you through. It feels like you are all alone and there is no evidence of God's presence. Even when you can't feel it or see it God is working and there is a tiny cloud on the horizon. God is sending you rain. Fresh cleansing rain will be falling soon and you will thrive again. Intimacy will be renewed. **Acts 3:19 (KJV)** *¹⁹Repent ye therefore, and be converted, that your sins may be blotted out, when the times of refreshing shall come from the presence of the Lord;* Now just so no one gets all condemned and thinks that a dry season means you have sinned just forget that. Repentance is not always about sin. The word repentance means to turn around and walk in the opposite direction. Sometimes it is just a new cry from the heart saying we really do want God; it is that acknowledgement that says we were casual about our relationship. Sometimes passion grew lighter than it used to be and we didn't do anything to change it. We might stay in that indifferent place until that becomes our norm. If that is the case, we need to turn around and renew our aim. We need to see Him instead of our dryness. "To be cross-conscious is to see Jesus, who loves you so much that He willingly died for you on the cross. To be cross-conscious is to look to Jesus who offered His own body to be punished; so that your body can be free from all punishment...it is to fix your eyes on Jesus who has provided for your deliverance and victory at the cross." (Prince 1/31/20)

Worship music is one of my ways back. For me just going into a service where there is real worship starts whetting my appetite for more of Him. If I really need a fresh anointing, and I have been walking in dry places, I play love songs to the Lord that minister to my spirit. I cry out with the lyrics to Jesus Culture singing <u>Let it Rain</u>. Right now I am listening to Elevation Worship singing, <u>There is a Cloud</u>. With every word my heart says fill up every dry crevice and flood all my empty places and saturate my soul afresh. It might feel awesome, or not. The point is I make my way back to passion on purpose. I turn around and refocus. I believe, even if that cloud is just the size of a man's hand; He will shower me with His loving presence again. I know it in very core of my being, so I don't let circumstances or feelings control me for long. There really are times of refreshing that come from the presence of the Lord and I find those times of refreshing while standing in the sanctuary of my church or the family room in the basement of my house. I might find them in the car while I drive, but I look to Him and Jesus is always there. I start aiming for His heart again, and I find His love reaching for me.

He is there for you too. You don't always feel Him. You might not always see His hand at work but you can trust His heart is for you. He loves you passionately. He is seeking you far more than you are seeking Him. All He wants is for you to look towards the sky and ask for rain. He has a storm brewing that will soak you with love and get you back on track. It is not the heart that never wavers, but the one that ultimately looks to God, that pleases Him. It is a simple turning toward His face that gets our aim right on target. God wants a heart that will keep looking up. One that will apply that generous blood poured out from our Savior, over and over until we are clean and free and ready for Him to carry us afresh.

The Lyrics to Elevation Worship's song <u>There is a Cloud</u>, say "Hear the Word roaring as thunder, with a new future to tell. For the dry season is over. There is a cloud beginning to swell...We offer our heart...We receive your rain." Keep those words rolling around in your spirit. Keep the scripture in front of your eyes. Even when you don't feel like it, press on in prayer and worship.

That flood is on the way, rushing over everything in its path. Nothing is the same after a flood. In 1993, there was a serious flood in our area. It moved trees that were deeply rooted; it washed houses off their foundations. That flood cut new paths for the river that are still there today. Nothing was able to withstand the floodwaters when they came. **Isaiah 59:19 (KJV)** *[19] So shall they fear the name of the LORD from the west, and his glory from the rising of the sun. When the enemy shall come in like a flood, the Spirit of the LORD shall lift up a standard against him.* Know this; there was no punctuation in the original Hebrew text. I read it like this when the enemy comes, then like a flood God raises up a defense for us. God stands between us and every attack, emotional or physical or spiritual. When God comes in like a flood, depression will yield to it. Every dry place is made new and the water will level out those ruts in your life. There is a cloud on the horizon. Cling to the promise of rain. I hear the sound of abundance of rain too. Say it, sing it, and believe it. You will see it. Once you are past the dry season, you will get your aim right on target.

Hebrews 12:2 (KJV) *² Looking unto Jesus the author and finisher of our faith; who for the joy that was set before him endured the cross, despising the shame, and is set down at the right hand of the throne of God.*

Looking unto Jesus

I was watching a movie where the actor was supposedly learning to shoot a rifle. Every time he pulled the trigger he shut his eyes. It was like he was bracing himself against the sound and the recoil of the weapon. Needless to say, he did not hit his target.

If we close our eyes we will always miss the mark. It doesn't matter if we are shooting a gun on the shooting range, or an arrow towards a target or if we are trying to stand in faith, we can only be on target if we are looking right at the bullseye. In our case we have to look at Jesus. We have to see Him before we see anything else. We have to put Him directly in our line of sight so we are not distracted by whatever else might come along.

Hebrews 12:2-3 (KJV) *² Looking unto Jesus the author and finisher of our faith; who for the joy that was set before him endured the cross, despising the shame, and is set down at the right hand of the throne of God. ³ For consider him that endured such contradiction of sinners against himself, lest ye be wearied and faint in your minds.* When faced with our daily challenges and temptations and even our life of service, we must keep looking at Jesus. We have to see Him who loved us so very much. We have to remember what He did for us and how He has changed our nature. We need to see His strength and presence as enough to overcome anything. We have to keep our eyes on the empty cross and the empty tomb and know that the same One who faced death and overcame it lives in us. We need to hold tight to that relationship. He sees all of our potential and has provided all that we need to reach it. **Philippians 1:6 (KJV)** *⁶ Being confident of this very thing, that he which hath begun a good work in you will perform it until the day of Jesus Christ:*

His love was boundless and His compassion moved Him to minister to us. **Ephesians 2:4-10 (KJV)** *⁴ But God, who is rich in mercy, for his great love wherewith he loved us, ⁵ Even when we* *were dead in sins, hath quickened us together with Christ, (by grace ye are saved;) ⁶And hath raised us up together, and made us sit together in heavenly places in Christ Jesus: ⁷That in the ages to come he might shew the exceeding riches of his grace in his kindness toward us through Christ Jesus.⁸ For by grace are ye saved through faith; and that not of yourselves: it is the gift of God: ⁹Not of works, lest any man should boast. ¹⁰ For we are his workmanship, created in Christ Jesus unto good works, which God hath before ordained that we should walk in them.* God intends for us to reflect His love and image to the world. Most of us gather with other believers and use our corporate abilities to minister, but ministry alone is missing the mark. It is not about being a big church or just touching the community. We are here to represent His love to the world. We can only reflect that love if we walk in relationship with Him.

We can get so used to "Church" that we start to think it is about us. Jesus is supposed to be the center of our focus. When we come together as a body of believers, we come united by the fact that we are all born again. We come to hear His word and sing His praise, and remember His sacrifice. We come alive because we are in Him and His love makes us one. But sometimes we think about our needs and our wants and our place in this organism that is His body. We can get the focus on what God can do for us instead of the fact that we are in the middle of a love story He wrote.

We can be right in the church building in the middle of a service and still miss the mark. I have heard people say, "I love the preaching and the people and the outreach your church does, but my kids need more social programs so I am going to look for a church that offers a big youth group and more social activities." When parents place emphasis on activities and lots of other kids to surround theirs they are missing the mark. They are looking in the natural while their children could end up in a popular group and still unsaved. They are not truly looking at what matters eternally as much as what seems important to them now. Those who seek what is easy or enjoyable at the cost of the anointing have lost focus.

Sometimes even well intentioned believers can get off target. Our church has anointed worship, but some people are looking for concert level music; they want entertainment more than real worship. God never asked us for perfection on the platform. God never intended that worship be so scripted that it does not flow naturally. What He wants is for us to allow the music to draw us nearer to Him. Worship is our time to honor Him and pour out our love on Him.

Have you ever had one of those songs that used to really bless you and then it was sung so much that you got tired of it? My dear friend, Donna, got a wakeup call one day when the worship leader started playing <u>Shout to the Lord</u>. She was thinking that she was just tired of that song. She was singing but definitely not worshipping. When her attitude was showing she heard in her spirit, "They aren't singing it to you." That got her a real quick attitude adjustment. She never looks at it as song service now, it is not entertainment and it is not for us. She sees that portion of the service as our time to minister to the One we love and she truly worships Him. No song is on a black list, she chooses to focus on God no matter what tune or lyrics; the song is from the heart. Looking at Him makes all the difference.

Philippians 3:13-14 (KJV) *[13] Brethren, I count not myself to have apprehended: but this one thing I do, forgetting those things which are behind, and reaching forth unto those things which are before, [14] I press toward the mark for the prize of the high calling of God in Christ Jesus.*

Where are you in the crowd?

When I study the Bible, I try to see the events from various places. I imagine being different characters in the story so I can feel what they might have felt. I try not to be a casual outside observer.

You might not have thought about it much but Jesus was always surrounded by people. There were times He sent out twelve disciples and times He sent out seventy so they had to be following along with the masses. There were women who ministered to Him that traveled with the Lord, like Mary Magdalene and at times the mother of Jesus. There was a least one wealthy wife of a prominent man who gave freely to His ministry.

In any crowd there were the curious, the honest seekers, the political and religious leaders who watched for the sake of retaining their power and title. There were frequently sick, needy, lost and demented souls who hoped for His help. Who were you? Where did you stand? Were you just pushed along by the crowd, invisible because there were so many other faces there or were you pressing in to get close to Him?

Mark 5:21-24 (KJV) *21 And when Jesus was passed over again by ship unto the other side, much people gathered unto him: and he was nigh unto the sea. 22 And, behold, there cometh one of the rulers of the synagogue, Jairus by name; and when he saw him, he fell at his feet, 23 And besought him greatly, saying, My little daughter lieth at the point of death: I pray thee, come and lay thy hands on her, that she may be healed; and she shall live. 24 And Jesus went with him; and much people followed him, and thronged him.* It cost Jairus to come. He was blowing up his public reputation. He was rejecting the laws and the synagogue where he was respected; in essence he just resigned a very lucrative career. He placed all his faith and hope in this miracle man he had probably never met. He was leaving his sick daughter's side to run for help to this prophet and teacher. Those could have easily been the last few moments he could hold her and shower her with loving words. Jairus chose to leave her to get to the Rabbi from Nazareth. He was asking for a miracle and his very actions said that he believed Jesus could and would help. He was declaring by his actions that this was the Messiah. He threw everything else away to get to Jesus and cry out for mercy. Jesus agreed to come, and they started off towards Jairus' house. It is hard to travel fast in a crowd. I am sure Jairus wanted to ask people to move out of the way but somehow, knowing his own need he did not discredit or dishonor theirs. Jesus was going with him. They were walking slowly towards his sick daughter when along comes another need, a holy interruption.

Mark 5:24-28 (KJV) *[24] And Jesus went with him; and much people followed him, and thronged him. [25] And a certain woman, which had an issue of blood twelve years,* she had been critically ill for the entire life of Jairus' daughter. *[26] And had suffered many things of many physicians, and had spent all that she had, and was nothing bettered, but rather grew worse,* She was physically, and emotionally and financially bankrupt; there was no more hope in medicine or doctors. *[27] When she had heard of Jesus, came in the press behind, and touched his garment. [28] For she said, If I may touch but his clothes, I shall be whole.* She wasn't just hoping to brush up alongside of the Lord; she was reaching out intentionally for the hem of His garment, that boarder as Luke recorded it. There was a promise of divine healing in the Word of God and that blue thread in the corner of the Rabbi's garment, His tallit, was symbolic of that promise. She risked a lot to come. Women were socially forbidden to touch any man other than their own family members. And not only was she a woman in a man's world, she was a sick, bleeding woman. For her to touch anyone even casually was to make them ceremonially unclean. She was basically on the same level as a leper; she was forbidden to come within several feet of any person. She was supposed to cover her mouth and cry out unclean in a loud voice so no one would accidentally be contaminated by her. She is weak; her illness has lasted for twelve years. It is difficult, but she pushes past onlookers and if need be she crawls towards the master and reaches out for the hem of His garment. She reached out for more than the linen cloth. When she takes hold of that tassel by faith, she is claiming all the Old Testament promises of healing from Isaiah 53 and Psalms 103. She is taking hold of the God of Abraham and Isaac and Jacob. Everything in her was reaching for the Word who became flesh [John 1:1]. **Mark 5:29-34 (KJV)** *29 And straightway the fountain of her blood was dried up; and she felt in her body that she was healed of that plague.* Faith works! *30 And Jesus, immediately knowing in himself that virtue had gone out of him, turned him about in the press, and said, Who touched my clothes?* He stopped. The crowd halted. Jairus is still concerned for his daughter, she is near the point of death, but Jesus stopped to ask who touched Him. *31 And his disciples said unto him, Thou seest the multitude thronging thee, and sayest thou, Who touched me? 32 And he looked round about to see her that had done this thing.* She had tried to take the blessing unnoticed. She could have been stoned for what she did, so admitting it was dangerous. When He stopped and looked at her, she could not deny Him, would not hide in the crowd. *33 But the woman fearing and trembling, knowing what was done in her, came and fell down before him, and told him all the truth. 34 And he said unto her, Daughter, thy faith hath made thee whole; go in peace, and be whole of thy plague.* That woman was not the only one who took healing by reaching out to touch the tassel of His Tallit. **Matthew 14:35-36 (KJV)** *35 And when the men of that place had knowledge of him, they sent out into all that country round about, and brought unto him all that were diseased; 36 And besought him that they might only touch the hem of his garment: and as many as touched were made perfectly whole.* Like all of those others she reached out in faith and was healed. How awesome for her, but time was passing and death claimed that little girl. While this woman gained life, it drained from the beloved daughter of Jairus.

Mark 5:35-43 (KJV) *35 While he yet spake, there came from the ruler of the synagogue's house certain which said, Thy daughter is dead: why troublest thou the Master any further? 36 As soon as Jesus heard the word that was spoken, he saith unto the ruler of the synagogue, Be not afraid, only believe. 37 And he suffered no man to follow him, save Peter, and James, and John the brother of James. 38 And he cometh to the house of the ruler of the synagogue, and seeth the tumult, and them that wept and wailed greatly. 39 And when he was come in, he saith unto them, Why make ye this ado, and weep? the damsel is not dead, but sleepeth. 40 And they laughed him to scorn. But when he had put them all out, he taketh the father and the mother of the damsel, and them that were with him, and entereth in where the damsel was lying.* There were three disciples that left the crowds behind to follow Jesus into that room, and there were family members pushed aside and left outside of that room. Faith and love working hand in hand allowed only a few to see the whole of the miracle. Many were ineligible to enter the room. There were curious and fearful and distraught people in the crowd. There were Pharisees who having heard the woman's confession ran home to bathe and change clothes because they could have been touched by her and defiled. Where were you? *41 And he took the damsel by the hand, and said unto her, Talitha cumi; which is, being interpreted, Damsel, I say unto thee, arise.* Jesus spoke to her like her mother and father would have when waking her in the morning. *42 And straightway the damsel arose, and walked; for she was of the age of twelve years. And they were astonished with a great astonishment. 43 And he charged them straitly that no man should know it; and commanded that something should be given her to eat.*

Remember that there is still a crowd outside. There are angry people and fearful and happy people and some that are just a little nosey wanting to see what happened. There was a healed woman who was rejoicing in her new strength and hoping for the girl to live. When Jesus left there, some continued to follow and some veered off. New followers joined the mob. It is hard to remain neutral and impartial to the events you witness. Some of the things He said were insulting, challenging, the crowds as a whole did not accept them.

It is always an individual call to follow Him. It is always personal and costly. **Matthew 7:21-23 (KJV)** *²¹ Not every one that saith unto me, Lord, Lord, shall enter into the kingdom of heaven; but he that doeth the will of my Father which is in heaven. ²² Many will say to me in that day, Lord, Lord, have we not prophesied in thy name? and in thy name have cast out devils? and in thy name done many wonderful works? ²³ And then will I profess unto them, I never knew you: depart from me, ye that work iniquity.* They were happy to see the miracles and hear the parables, but did they really know Him? No! Just like now, some people go to church and enjoy it, but they aren't really after His heart. Not everyone wants to be intimately acquainted with the Lord.

Luke 14:25-27 (KJV) *²⁵ And there went great multitudes with him: and he turned, and said unto them, ²⁶ If any man come to me, and hate not his father, and mother, and wife, and children, and brethren, and sisters, yea, and his own life also, he cannot be my disciple. ²⁷ And whosoever doth not bear his cross, and come after me, cannot be my disciple.* "If anyone…That is a fairly inclusive word. Jesus isn't laying out the entrance requirements for the twelve disciples. He is not addressing a group of pastors and missionaries. What Jesus says is true for anyone who wants to follow Him." (Idleman p. 56) I know Jesus wants us to love everyone and hate no one, but in that culture to become a follower of Christ meant you were dead to all of them. You had to love Him more than anyone or anything else; to choose to follow Him would cost you every other important thing and person in your life. "A decision to follow Jesus would have been interpreted as turning your back on your family and walking away from them." (Idleman p. 57)

Not everything Jesus said or did was popular with the crowds. Some of His sayings offended them. When He told them they had to become one with Him, to be completely dependent upon Him, some rejected His teaching. **John 6:47-59 (KJV)** ⁴⁷

Verily, verily, I say unto you, He that believeth on me hath everlasting life. [48] *I am that bread of life.* [49] *Your fathers did eat manna in the wilderness, and are dead.* [50] *This is the bread which cometh down from heaven, that a man may eat thereof, and not die.* [51] *I am the living bread which came down from heaven: if any man eat of this bread, he shall live forever: and the bread that I will give is my flesh, which I will give for the life of the world* [52] *The Jews therefore strove among themselves, saying, How can this man give us his flesh to eat?* [53] *Then Jesus said unto them, Verily, verily, I say unto you, Except ye eat the flesh of the Son of man, and drink his blood, ye have no life in you.* [54] *Whoso eateth my flesh, and drinketh my blood, hath eternal life; and I will raise him up at the last day.* [55] *For my flesh is meat indeed, and my blood is drink indeed.* [56] *He that eateth my flesh, and drinketh my blood, dwelleth in me, and I in him.* [57] *As the living Father hath sent me, and I live by the Father: so he that eateth me, even he shall live by me.* [58] *This is that bread which came down from heaven: not as your fathers did eat manna, and are dead: he that eateth of this bread shall live forever.*
[59] *These things said he in the synagogue, as he taught in Capernaum.*

They heard Jesus say that He was the bread of life. The crowds heard Jesus asking for full commitment. **John 6:60-69 (KJV)** [60] *Many therefore of his disciples, when they had heard this, said, This is an hard saying; who can hear it?* [61] *When Jesus knew in himself that his disciples murmured at it, he said unto them, Doth this offend you?* [62] *What and if ye shall see the Son of man ascend up where he was before?* [63] *It is the spirit that quickeneth; the flesh profiteth nothing: the words that I speak unto you, they are spirit, and they are life.* [64] *But there are some of you that believe not. For Jesus knew from the beginning who they were that believed not, and who should betray him.* [65] *And he said, Therefore said I unto you, that no man can come unto me, except it were given unto him of my Father.* [66] *From that time many of his disciples went back, and walked no more with him.* [67] *Then said Jesus unto the twelve, Will ye also go away?* [68] *Then Simon Peter answered him, Lord, to whom shall we go? thou hast the words of eternal* life. *⁶⁹And we believe and are sure that thou art that Christ, the Son of the living God.*

Many walked away, but Peter chose to press in. Even when it cost him his livelihood to follow, Peter climbed out of his boat, lay down his nets and went. Peter committed before he spoke to his wife. **Matthew 6:24 (KJV)** *²⁴No man can serve two masters: for either he will hate the one, and love the other; or else he will hold to the one, and despise the other. Ye cannot serve God and mammon.* Loving and serving the Lord means He owns all of you. Your time and money and reputation are all His. Jairus understood that, Peter understood that, but many in the crowd were casual followers. They could become offended and turn aside at any moment.

Matthew 16:15 (KJV) *¹⁵He saith unto them, But whom say ye that I am?* What does your life story say of who He is? So where are you in that crowd? Are you the woman with faith and determination to touch Him? Are you the one who walks on knowing that your very reason for walking lies dead at home? Are you the one who hears Jesus say not to fear, only believe and without any tangible evidence you turn and start walking back to face death with the Healer at your side? Are you the one who laying aside all else seeks Him, and regardless of the cost you will follow? You just might be the one seeking for the very heart of God. Not everyone who heard Him say, "Follow me" went all the way to the cross with Jesus.

Paul was not present to see all those miracles any more than you or I was there. While we can imagine ourselves among the crowd, we did not see it first-hand. And yet like Paul, God made Himself known to us and gave us the opportunity to decide to follow. Paul said he was unworthy and yet Jesus took him in; me too. Paul wrote so much of what we follow as Christians today. Paul was recognized as a leader in the church. From his prison cell he wrote this. **Philippians 3:13-14 (KJV)** *¹³Brethren, I count not myself to have apprehended: but this one thing I do, forgetting those things which are behind, and reaching forth unto* *those things which are before,* ¹⁴ *I press toward the mark for the prize of the high calling of God in Christ Jesus.*

Maybe it is good for us from time to time to look and see where we are in the crowd and to determine to press in a little closer. The call of Jesus "Follow Me" might appear to be spoken into the faceless masses. But it is directed to individuals. Jesus calls for us to personally aim at the center of God's will and follow more closely than before.

Philippians 4:5-7 (KJV) *⁵ Let your moderation be known unto all men. The Lord is at hand. ⁶ Be careful for nothing; but in everything by prayer and supplication with thanksgiving let your requests be made known unto God. ⁷ And the peace of God, which passeth all understanding, shall keep your hearts and minds through Christ Jesus.*

Don't worry—Pray

Why is it that fear and doubt and worry come so easily to people? I have noticed that deep concern takes its toll on those who focus on what might be or could be or is about to happen. You can either worry or pray. The two do not mix well; you are either walking in fear or in faith.

I remember hearing this story from the viewpoint of a tiny mouse who crept into various houses. Maggie said unto her friend Molly, "What are you staring at?" Molly said, "I am just wondering? "You see all these people working and scurrying about, why do they fret so?" "Whatever do you mean," said Maggie? "Well," began Molly, "they are in a constant state of worry or fear or even panic. They wake up early and stay up late, and all day long they struggle against the world about them. They face everything as if they will not have enough. They dread meeting strangers, and fear what others think. They talk about what has not even occurred. They fear the weather and yet they have homes for shelter. They plant a crop and then assume it will not produce. They have closets full of clothing and yet seek and seek for ways to get more. They have fitful sleep and stockpile and greedily compete one with another. What do you suppose makes them so?" Maggie replied, "It must be that they do not have a loving Father like we do. We have never been fearful or worried. We know that our Father will provide all that we need…It's too bad they don't have a Father like us." Maggie understood that the Heavenly Father provided for her every need. Maybe the people she watched did not understand that they, too, could rest in the provision of a loving God.

Jesus taught the same story with a little less animation. **Luke 12:22-31 (KJV)** *²²And he said unto his disciples, Therefore I* *say unto you, Take no thought for your life, what ye shall eat; neither for the body, what ye shall put on.* ²³ *The life is more than meat, and the body is more than raiment* ²⁴ *Consider the ravens: for they neither sow nor reap; which neither have storehouse nor barn; and God feedeth them: how much more are ye better than the fowls?* ²⁵ *And which of you with taking thought can add to his stature one cubit?* ²⁶ *If ye then be not able to do that thing which is least, why take ye thought for the rest?* ²⁷ *Consider the lilies how they grow: they toil not, they spin not; and yet I say unto you, that Solomon in all his glory was not arrayed like one of these.* ²⁸ *If then God so clothe the grass, which is to day in the field, and tomorrow is cast into the oven; how much more will he clothe you, O ye of little faith?* ²⁹ *And seek not ye what ye shall eat, or what ye shall drink, neither be ye of doubtful mind.* ³⁰ *For all these things do the nations of the world seek after: and your Father knoweth that ye have need of these things.* ³¹ *But rather seek ye the kingdom of God; and all these things shall be added unto you.* There is something about having a quiet confidence in the One who loves us best.

When faced with the challenges of life we have a choice to make. We can either worry or we can pray, putting our trust in the God who loves us. Once it is in His hands, we can walk away, without a care.

I had already been expecting to write about prayer and trust today. Then this morning my daily devotional said this. "A church member, after undergoing a mammogram, found that she had lumps in her breast. Upon receiving the doctor's report, she wrote this down on the report: Jesus is my healer. I receive my healing. I am healed. I rest in God completely." (Prince 1/8/20) This doesn't really sound like formal prayer. She took the negative report and just added a few lines of faith and trust in the God who heals. That lines up very well with the scripture. **James 1:6 (KJV)** ⁶ *But let him ask in faith, nothing wavering.* She might have formally prayed, that was not stated, but regardless she took her hands off of the situation. **I Peter 5:6-7 (KJV)** ⁶ *Humble yourselves therefore under the mighty hand of God, that he may* *exalt you in due time:* ⁷ *Casting all your care upon him; for he careth for you.*

"She was due back at the clinic later the same day for a biopsy to see if the lumps were malignant. Her sister-in-law, who was having lunch with her that day, witnessed her cheerful and worry-free attitude while she ate." "Back at the clinic, this precious sister sat among other ladies who were also there for their biopsies. They looked very worried, so she started sharing Jesus with them and prayed for some of them. When her turn came and she had an ultrasound scan done, the doctor was puzzled—her scan showed no evidence of any lumps!" (Prince 1/8/20) Those doctors called it a miracle.

"My friend, when you worry, you are actually believing that the devil has the power to make inroads into your life that God cannot protect you from. But when you refuse to worry, you are putting your faith in God. You have more confidence in His love and power working for you than in the devil's ability to harm you! When you refuse to worry, but choose to rest in the finished work of Christ, you will see the manifestation of your blessing. You will see your miracle!" (Prince 1/8/20) You can totally trust that God hears and answers prayer. Put your problems in His hands and then let go.

Philippians 4:6-7 (KJV) ⁶ *Be careful for nothing; but in everything by prayer and supplication with thanksgiving let your requests be made known unto God.* ⁷ *And the peace of God, which passeth all understanding, shall keep your hearts and minds through Christ Jesus.*

Just pray. I don't know why we make prayer such a task. Prayer was always meant to be a conversation between God and His loved ones. It is a simple act of communication, a joining in harmony with God. It is the place where we share all that is important to us with someone who cares about our needs. Just talk to Him.

There should be no fear in approaching God. He is holy, but He is also your Father. God loves you and longs for time with you. He wants you to talk with Him, not just at Him. While it is true that He knows your needs before you ask, it is precious to Him that you would bring them to Him. He wants to hear the story from your perspective, and then He wants to elevate it to His. When we see it in comparison to His provision the problem shrinks.

I Thessalonians 5:16-18 (KJV) *[16] Rejoice evermore. [17] Pray without ceasing. [18] In everything give thanks: for this is the will of God in Christ Jesus concerning you.* If we take every care to Him, we can rejoice all the time. We have a very powerful, very loving Father who wants to be intimately involved in our lives. So much peace is available to us, if we will just let Him handle things for us. Most of us are like two year olds, constantly saying, "I want to do it." When my Great grandson says that and takes his shoestrings in hand, I am relatively sure that he won't tie them but there will be a serious knot to undo before I can tie them. Honestly it saves a lot of mess and frustration if we just put it in the hands of the One who is able.

Some people are a little self-conscious when it comes to prayer. For some reason they are all tied up in the words and forget that it is just conversation. To be honest I have friends that tremble at the thought of praying out loud. When the disciples asked Jesus for a way to pray, He gave them a pattern to follow. **Matthew 6:9-13 (KJV)** *[9] After this manner therefore pray ye: Our Father which art in heaven, Hallowed be thy name. [10] Thy kingdom come. Thy will be done in earth, as it is in heaven. [11] Give us this day our daily bread. [12] And forgive us our debts, as we forgive our debtors. [13] And lead us not into temptation, but deliver us from evil: For thine is the kingdom, and the power, and the glory, forever. Amen.*

Let's just look at that for a minute. First of all, in the scriptures just prior to these, Jesus said when you pray, not if you pray. Jesus implied that we would talk with God. He also indicated that we should be real with God. Then He gave them the pattern, not a quotation to repeat. He said to look at the various parts of your conversation with the Father like this. **Matthew 6:9-13 (KJV)** *9 After this manner therefore pray ye: Our Father which art in heaven, Hallowed be thy name.* Honor your Father, start with worship, but lean on the relationship. He who is your Father; the King of the Universe is also your Abba, your Daddy, who loves you. Before you ask for your needs, pour out your love on Him. *10 Thy kingdom come. Thy will be done in earth, as it is in heaven.* Recognize that it is His kingdom and His will that matter and align yourself with His Word and His will. Put His plans before your own. When Jesus was in the Garden of Gethsemane, He said, "*Not my will but yours be done.*" Jesus purchased your salvation by a huge sacrifice rather than taking the easy way out. He asked for what pleased the Father rather than what was comfortable or convenient. Yielding to God's will on earth creates a perfect sense of peace within the believer. There is no lack or need in heaven, there is no strife or fear or sickness. There is no death in heaven. God's will on earth as in heaven is a restful place. God's will is always better than mine. Then, with the big picture in mind, ask for what you need. *11 Give us this day our daily bread.* Ask in faith, trusting Him to supply or change your desire. God knows my tomorrow, so I think His plan will work out fine for me. Notice it says daily bread. God will put it in our hands when we need it, but we might not have it well in advance. Just like when God provided manna in the wilderness. It fell day by day as needed. Jesus called himself the bread of life, so in a way asking for daily bread is asking for Him, His presence and provision are tied together. Jesus was saying that you can never survive a day without Him but partaking of Him one day at a time satisfies. Give us this day our daily bread covers food, but it also provides for every need spiritual, physical, and financial. *12 And forgive us our debts, as we forgive our debtors.* When we recognize the enormous sin debt that God has forgiven, we are more likely to forgive others generously too. We love because He loved. We forgive as an act of our will because He forgave. It is not so hard when we see from that perspective. *13 And lead us not into temptation, but deliver us from evil:* Lord protect me from every influence and trap of the enemy. *For thine is the kingdom, and the power, and the glory, forever. Amen.* The prayer comes full circle when we go back to thanksgiving and worship. Having prayed we trust. Knowing that He is in control we have great peace and joy. **John 14:27 (KJV)** [27] *Peace I leave with you, my peace I give unto you: not as the world giveth, give I unto you. Let not your heart be troubled, neither let it be afraid.* He said you decide to trust. You do not let your heart be troubled. You take hold of His peace. You stop fear in its tracks.

Prayer is not so hard when we come the way children do. God I love you and I know I need you. Here is what is bothering me; here is the need of my sister. Lord I know you love me, so I trust you to handle it. Thank you. That prayer is right on target.

Romans 15:13 (KJV) [13] *Now the God of hope fill you with all joy and peace in believing, that ye may abound in hope, through the power of the Holy Ghost.* So don't worry, pray, and that will keep your focus on the God who answers.

Acts 15:16-17 (KJV) *¹⁶After this I will return, and will build again the tabernacle of David, which is fallen down; and I will build again the ruins thereof, and I will set it up: ¹⁷That the residue of men might seek after the Lord, and all the Gentiles, upon whom my name is called, saith the Lord, who doeth all these things.*

Unashamed Passion

If David was a man after God's own heart what else is there in his life to follow? David was a worshiper. He wrote most of the Psalms. They were simple songs of adoration to the God he knew and loved.

In his book, <u>God's Favorite House</u>, Tommy Tenney focuses almost entirely on intimate worship. **Acts 15:16-17 (KJV)** *16 After this I will return, and will build again the tabernacle of David, which is fallen down; and I will build again the ruins thereof, and I will set it up: 17 That the residue of men might seek after the Lord, and all the Gentiles, upon whom my name is called, saith the Lord, who doeth all these things.* God wanted a place where there was intimacy. He was not concerned about the gold and tapestry that hung in Solomon's temple. God did not long for the ritual and ceremony of formal worship. What God wanted was the time when He and David were near one another. God wanted "A rebirth of the passion that caused it to be built in the first place. David's tabernacle was less structure and more of an event." (Tenney p. 4) God didn't just want a nice house, He wanted a real home. Just like ours, God's favorite house is one filled with memories. "If the passion of David's heart can be restored, then God Himself will assist in the rebuilding process of the tabernacle. He said so!" (Tenney p. 4)

David constructed a tent, mostly just a tarp and some poles it was nothing compared to the glory of the Tabernacle of Moses or the Temple, but it was a place of real worship. David was hungry for the presence of God. He wanted to bring the Ark of the Covenant into Jerusalem. He did not care for it as a symbol or treat it like an idol; neither did he look at the value of the gold that covered that box. He was not enamored with the jar of manna or the stone tablets that were inside. He wanted God! "He was interested in the blue flame that hovered between the outstretched wings of the cherubim on top of the ark. That is what he wanted, because there was something about the flame that signified that God Himself was present. And wherever that glory of that manifested presence of God went, there was victory, power and blessing. Intimacy will bring about the blessing, but the pursuit of blessing won't always bring about intimacy." (Tenney p. 7) David was indeed a man hungering after a heart that is like God's heart. It was his desire that was most important. It was his passion that impressed God, not his position as king, not his wealth, and certainly not his actions, God saw that David was looking for more presence and that touched the heart of God.

God was willing to be revealed to the heart that sought Him. "The ark, the mercy seat and the blue flame of God's presence were always hidden behind the thick fabric of the veil…God never liked that separation…God was the one who ripped the veil from top to bottom in the temple of Herod in Jerusalem." (Tenney p. 8) God wanted to be face to face with man, and when Jesus hung on the cross His very flesh was torn, throwing open the most holy place and allowing man access into the glorious presence of God. "The only thing encircling God's presence in David's tabernacle were the worshipers who ministered to Him 24 hours a day." King David could hear the singing and "He could look toward the hillside adjacent to his quarters and see the shadows of shuffling feet dancing around the ark, illuminated by the flickering of candlelight and lamps." (Tenney p. 9) Tenney said it was almost as if the outstretched arms of worshiper were hold open the heavens, keeping the blessing there. He said David was looking at the glory through dancing feet and outstretched arms and he was seeing the One he loved. Not only that, but a beggar on the street or a merchant or even the smallest of children had a view into the very presence of God. There were no barriers hiding God from men. God wanted the house of David rebuilt because he wants us to know the intimacy that is available to each of us. God and man both hunger for a place of easy access where there is nothing that hides the one from the other.

I didn't live in the time of tabernacles and the Ark of God's presence but I do understand unashamed hunger and real worship. I remember the sinful woman who anointed the Lord in Luke chapter 7 and I want to be more like her.

Luke 7:36-39 (KJV) *36 And one of the Pharisees desired him that he would eat with him. And he went into the Pharisee's house, and sat down to meat.* By all accounts Simon was probably a decent man. He was a Pharisee so he knew the law and probably kept it. He was better prepared to stand before God than most of the men in town. He was somewhat wealthy and though he did not honor Jesus as the Christ, he was at least curious about this teacher. *37 And, behold, a woman in the city, which was a sinner, when she knew that Jesus sat at meat in the Pharisee's house, brought an alabaster box of ointment, 38 And stood at his feet.* She was most likely a prostitute. The name they called her was much stronger than I would be comfortable saying. It carried with it shame and humiliation that we cannot comprehend. Here she is in the very presence of the Son of God. The contrast was lost on no one. It was scandalous to everyone in the room that she would come in there uninvited, unwelcome, and of shameful reputation. She just walked up to Jesus and touched Him. He never withdrew from her touch. The only one who had a right to judge her was the Lord. He was also the only one who was not offended. She had not always been dirty and vile; there was a time she was someone's little girl. She had long since lost her reputation and her virtue. She is no longer the one that people hold out hope for or dreams and plans for a future or family. It had been a long time since she was welcome in polite society. The whole room was full of men who despised her and she probably hated herself. The scripture says she just barged in but she also *brought an alabaster box of ointment.* That box and the perfume inside would cost about a year's wages. It was not a small offering. It is likely that she had used tiny amounts of this or a similar perfume in her profession. Women of disrepute often used rich perfumes and oils, and here she is, pouring out the whole of her shameful past in an act of worship that only a truly repentant heart can offer. She cried the whole time she ministered to the Lord. *38 And stood at His feet* *behind Him weeping, and began to wash His feet with tears, and did wipe them with the hairs of her head, and kissed His feet, and anointed them with the ointment.* Maybe she was thinking of how she had earned the money that bought that perfume, or maybe she remembered the cherished little girl she used to be and thought about how disgusting her life had become. She was probably pretty but men only looked at her with lust. No one looked at her heart and loved her for who she was inside. She was just a convenience for men who wanted her body for a few hours. Maybe she was thinking of how ugly her sin was and how much she wanted to be clean again. As she wept she did something unorthodox, she took down her hair. It was a violation of social custom for respectable women to do that, but she was not respectable. She had let down her hair many times as a prostitute, and each time it was another wound to her own heart and another scar and stain on her own soul. This time it was an act of homage, to dry the feet her tears had bathed. She let down her hair this one last time out of love and respect for the one man worthy of her love and admiration.

She wept and bathed His feet in her remorse. Her deep sorrow and shame overcame her. *38 And stood at his feet behind him weeping, and began to wash his feet with tears, and did wipe them with the hairs of her head, and kissed his feet, and anointed them with the ointment.* I can almost hear her heart cry out, when her tears hit His dirty feet. She was not only wiping away the dust and stench from the road, but maybe she thought her tears were too vile to touch Him. *39 Now when the Pharisee which had bidden him saw it, he spake within himself, saying, This man, if he were a prophet, would have known who and what manner of woman this is that toucheth him: for she is a sinner.* It had to take all her courage to walk in there knowing the whispers and stares she would encounter. She knew she was unwelcome, but she had to do what she came for. I am sure she stood behind the Lord because she feared to face this holy man. When she finally did look Jesus in the eyes, she saw only love and compassion. Simon had none of that for her. Simon did not esteem Jesus highly as even a prophet, and definitely not as the Messiah. He was waiting for Jesus to denounce and rebuke the woman but instead Jesus forgave her. He forgave us too.

Luke 7:40-50 (KJV) *⁴⁰And Jesus answering said unto him, Simon, I have somewhat to say unto thee. And he saith, Master, say on. ⁴¹There was a certain creditor which had two debtors: the one owed five hundred pence, and the other fifty. ⁴²And when they had nothing to pay, he frankly forgave them both. Tell me therefore, which of them will love him most? ⁴³Simon answered and said, I suppose that he, to whom he forgave most. And he said unto him, Thou hast rightly judged. ⁴⁴And he turned to the woman, and said unto Simon, Seest thou this woman?* Of course Simon could see her, but he did not look at her as Jesus did. Simon never saw the treasure within her. He quickly judged and dismissed her. Simon did not see Jesus either, not as she did. *I entered into thine house, thou gavest me no water for my feet: but she hath washed my feet with tears, and wiped them with the hairs of her head. ⁴⁵Thou gavest me no kiss: but this woman since the time I came in hath not ceased to kiss my feet. ⁴⁶My head with oil thou didst not anoint: but this woman hath anointed my feet with ointment.* In every household someone was designated to wash the feet of guests, usually the lowest servant. It was always customary to greet a friend or an honored guest with a kiss on both cheeks and to anoint them with inexpensive olive oil. It was common courtesy, but none of it was extended to the Lord in this house. They knelt down at the table with none of the customary washings or greetings. Simon had disrespected the Lord. *⁴⁷Wherefore I say unto thee, Her sins, which are many, are forgiven; for she loved much: but to whom little is forgiven, the same loveth little. ⁴⁸And he said unto her, Thy sins are forgiven. ⁴⁹And they that sat at meat with Him began to say within themselves, Who is this that forgiveth sins also? ⁵⁰And he said to the woman, Thy faith hath saved thee; go in peace.* For some reason Simon had invited Jesus come, but he did not honor Him as a prophet or even a teacher. In his pride, Simon thought he was better than any common sinner. Simon did not realize that he was as damaged as that disgraceful woman and he too needed forgiveness. I am sure he was outraged to think Jesus would honor a prostitute over him. That woman came in an attitude of true repentance and sorrow for her sin. She had determined to worship Jesus. She had come with a heart of unlimited devotion, and humble adoration. She had closed the door on her sordid past, and opened herself up to public outrage and a new social disgrace in order to minister to Jesus. She had placed herself at His feet. She had worshiped with abandon, and she was rewarded for her love.

Jesus saw that sad, broken woman differently from those who looked in the natural. He saw her as beloved by the Father, damaged beyond recognition by the world, but still valuable and beautiful to God. He saw her through the eyes of love. **I John 48-10 (KJV)** *⁸He that loveth not knoweth not God; for God is love. ⁹In this was manifested the love of God toward us, because that God sent his only begotten Son into the world, that we might live through him. ¹⁰Herein is love, not that we loved God, but that he loved us, and sent his Son to be the propitiation for our sins.* God loved her first and He loved us first and that motivated Him to save us.

Jesus never said that her sin did not matter; what He did say was that her sin was not going to stop His love. He became sin so that it could no longer hold her or any of us prisoner. Once years ago I played the part of that fallen woman. I knelt at the feet of the man who would later become my pastor and wiped his feet with my hair. I remember how real it all became to me. All of us are that dirty, broken one. We all come to Him with nothing more than the shattered pieces of our lives to offer. I remember that play practice so well, there was a moment of great awe. Tim and I were both crying, because we both felt the reality of the grace that Jesus offered that poor sinful woman, and us.

We would do well to kneel there at His feet, remembering that amazing grace God offered. "When is the last time you had a moment with Jesus like this woman in Luke 7 had? When's the last time you've poured yourself out before Him? When is the last time tears streamed down your face as you expressed your love for

Him? When is the last time you demonstrated your love for Him with reckless abandonment?" (Idleman p. 51)

Song of Songs 8:6 (KJV) *...for love is strong as death*; In fact love for mankind was so strong that it walked through the earth in the form of a man and overcame death. God's love is limitless. Even though man is dirty and worn and broken God still loves us. God is not against us, in fact, He is for us.

God is drawn to the heart of worship. He longs for fellowship more than we do. "God isn't attracted by the quality of our worship or our musical ability. It is because of who we are. He is attracted because of His relationship to the worshipers. We're His children." (Tenney p. 115)

It is very much like when my great grandchildren come running to me with their arms wide ready for an embrace and they say "Grammy I love you." When they come running, they throw up their hands knowing I will pick them up, and hold them close for as long as they want to be held, and then I will let them down to play. There is nothing that pleases me more. God wants us to lift our hands like they do, reaching out for Him with loving trust and devotion. I think when He sees us with outstretched hands, He wants to pick us up and hold us too.

Psalm 63:3-8 (KJV) *³ Because thy lovingkindness is better than life, my lips shall praise thee.⁴ Thus will I bless thee while I live: I will lift up my hands in thy name. ⁵ My soul shall be satisfied as with marrow and fatness; and my mouth shall praise thee with joyful lips: ⁶When I remember thee upon my bed, and meditate on thee in the night watches. ⁷ Because thou hast been my help, therefore in the shadow of thy wings will I rejoice. ⁸ My soul followeth hard after thee: thy right hand upholdeth me.*

Sometimes I when I read about that broken woman, I wonder, "Where is my alabaster box?" Dear Lord let my worship touch you and my tears run freely in honor of you. If I am embarrassed or abased so be it, but let me turn my whole heart to you and let me be fully surrendered to the one and only Lover of my soul. Let my words and actions and all that I am aim right for the heart of God. You are my target, my goal and all that I need and want is in you. I am throwing my hands in the air and saying Abba, Father, I love you.

Works Cited

Association, Reader's Digest. Readers Digest *Who's Who in the Bible – an Illustrated Biographical Dictionary*. (Pleasantville, NY: Readers Digest Association, 1994) p. 372.

Beacon Bible Commentary. (Kansas City, MO. Beacon Hill Press, 1969) vol. 2, p. 30

Hagin, Kenneth Jr., *Listen to Your Heart*. (Tulsa, OK, Rhema Bible Church, 1992) p.62.

Idleman, Kyle. *Not a Fan. Becoming a Completely Committed Follower of Jesus.* (Grand Rapids MI: Zondervan 2011) p.51, 56, 57.

Keller, Philip, *A Shepherd Looks at Psalm 23*. (New York, NY Inspirational Press, 1993) p. 41, 42.

Prince, Joseph, *Daily Grace Inspirations* (Joseph Prince Ministries 9/25/19, 10/19/19, 11/2/19, 1/8/20, 1/31/20.)

Tenney, Tommy. *God's Favorite House*. (Shippensburg, PA: Destiny Image Publishers, 2000) p. 4, 7, 8, 9, 115.

Rev. Kathryn L. Smith

Author Page

I was saved in 1972, in a revival at Suburban Baptist Church in Granite City IL. I learned to love the Lord and His Word and began my walk there. In 1980, I was filled with the Holy Spirit at Full Gospel Evangelistic Center of Alton. It was there that I began to minister the Word in Power. God called me to "Build up the body of Christ," and I have been preaching and teaching all these years for that purpose. Becoming an author was a natural expansion of that call to minister. I love teaching and preaching and there is no greater joy than walking the path He places before me. I serve locally as an associate minister at The House of Victory in Cottage Hills IL, under Pastor Timothy Naylor. I am available for speaking engagements and would gladly come minister at your church or conference.

Aiming for the Heart of God is my seventh book. If you were blessed by it, I would recommend that you read some of my others. There is Fire in the Blood, my first book, explores the blood sacrifices throughout time as they point to the Blood of Jesus and bring us the Fire of His presence. It was the same fire that fell on the sacrificial altars of Abel, Elijah, and Moses that produced the blaze of Pentecost. As we honor the blood and recognize its power we make way for the glory of God; if we want to experience the Fire, we know where to find it; 'There is Fire in the Blood.'

My second book, Meet Me on the Mountain, focuses on intimate fellowship with God. The mountain of God is that place where faith and hunger produce His presence. The drive to climb is not just man striving for God; it is an answer to the call. God loved us first and He is calling to the heart of man to draw nearer and stay longer in His presence. This book has more personal experiences included to demonstrate how He meets with us and longs for passionate fellowship with His children. If you seek Him—you will find Him.

My third book, I Hear the Rocks Falling was inspired by the woman caught in adultery and thrown at the feet of Jesus. She expected the stones to crush her. Instead she heard the sound of the rocks falling to the ground as her accusers left. Like her, most of us have had moments of despair and shame and condemnation. Repeated offences deepen our sense of loss, stacking one harsh, hardened, hurtful memory on top of another until we are bound within an internal prison. Jesus speaks to all of us to come out of those walls. We are to walk free from all condemnation and everything that has kept us tied to our past.

<u>Wilt Thou Be Made Whole</u> is an invitation to receive healing. On the cross, Jesus purchased salvation, and freedom from every consequence of Adam's fall. Healing belongs to us. It is not something we are trying to grasp; it was purchased for us by virtue of His broken body and shed blood. When we recognize that He bore our sickness like He bore our sin, we can access His healing power. Every word of testimony and scripture in this book was purposed to raise your faith so that you too can be free from sickness and disease. He is still asking, "Wilt Thou Be Made Whole?"

<u>I Am Who God Says I Am</u> is the fifth book that I have authored. This book helps us to see ourselves through our identity in Christ. We are loved and valued so much more than most of us know. I pray that you will learn to trust confidently in who God says you are.

<u>Starting with Zero</u> examines how God can use so much less to make so much more. We are insignificant in the whole of the universe without its Creator. God delights in taking us as we are and making us into what He alone could see all along. The devil would love to say are nothing but you have a destiny; you are an opportunity for God to make something that will bring Him glory.

Contact information:
Fire in the Blood Ministries
Rev. Kathryn L. Smith
Email: klssaved1972@yahoo.com
Fire in the Blood Ministries
also has a Facebook Page
fbm/revkathy   or   m.me/revkathy

Rev. Kathryn L. Smith

Rev. Kathryn L. Smith

www.ingramcontent.com/pod-product-compliance
Lightning Source LLC
Chambersburg PA
CBHW052151110526
44591CB00012B/1943